D1200589

Wimbledon

WIMB

Text by

Photographed by

LEDON

A Celebration

John McPhee

Alfred Eisenstaedt

New York ● The Viking Press

Other books by John McPhee

A Sense of Where You Are
The Headmaster
Oranges
The Pine Barrens
A Roomful of Hovings
Levels of the Game
The Crofter and the Laird
Encounters with the Archdruid

Other books by Alfred Eisenstaedt

Witness to Our Time
The Eye of Eisenstaedt
Martha's Vineyard
Witness to Nature

First published in 1972 by The Viking Press, Inc.
625 Madison Avenue, New York, N.Y. 10022

Published simultaneously in Canada by
The Macmillan Company of Canada Limited

SBN 670-77079-5

Library of Congress catalog card number: 71-182266

Printed in U.S.A.

Photographs Copyright © 1972 by Alfred Eisenstaedt

"Twynam of Wimbledon" is reprinted from *A Roomful of Hovings*, by John
McPhee, with permission of the publisher, Farrar, Straus & Giroux, Inc.
Copyright © 1968 by John McPhee. Originally published in *The New Yorker*.

"Hoad on Court 5" originally appeared in *Playboy* Magazine under the title
"Centre Court." Copyright © 1971 by John McPhee.

All rights reserved

We dedicate this book to

ROBERT TWYNAM

The authors wish to express their gratitude to Jim McManus, tennis player and photographer, who, between matches of his own, guided and assisted Alfred Eisenstaedt at Wimbledon. They are also most grateful to Nicolas Ducrot, who designed the book.

TABLE OF CONTENTS

AN INTRODUCTORY NOTE

In 1971, I went to Wimbledon after reading a manuscript written by John McPhee from notes he had made there in 1970. His details, for the most part, had been drawn from that tournament, but he did not even say who had won it. Instead, he had put together in words a series of glimpses that collectively spoke of the nature of the place, its appearance, the feelings in the air there, a sense of why Wimbledon had for so long been the focal moment of this game. The details—the stories about the players, the arrested fragments of the play—were of the sort that change but do not change. I went to Wimbledon to try to do the same with my camera.

I went remembering also a story John had written some years earlier about Robert Twynam, the extraordinary man who grows the Wimbledon grass. It was my privilege to spend almost a fortnight with this man in the place where he lives and works; and when I saw my photographs upon my return, I realized that Twynam's story had to be in the book as well.

Alfred Eisenstaedt

HOAD
ON COURT 5

Hoad on Court 5, weathered and leonine, has come from Spain, where he lives on his tennis ranch in the plains of Andalusia. Technically, he is an old hero trying a comeback, but, win or lose, for this crowd it is enough of a comeback that Hoad is here. There is tempestuous majesty in him, and people have congregated seven deep around his court just to feel the atmosphere there and to see him again. Hoad serves explosively, and the ball hits the fence behind his opponent without first intersecting the ground. His precision is off. The dead always rise slowly. His next serve splits the service line. Hoad is blasting some hapless Swiss into submission. As he tosses the ball up to serve again, all eyes lift above the court and the surrounding hedges, the green canvas fences, the beds of climbing roses, the ivy-covered walls—and at the top of the ball's parabola, it hangs for an instant in the sky against a background of half-timbered houses among plane trees and poplars on suburban hills. Rising from the highest hill is the steeple of St. Mary's Church, Wimbledon, where Hoad was married sixteen years ago. He swings through the ball and hits it very deep. "Fault." Hoad's wife, Jenny, and their several children are at the front of the crowd beside the court, watching with no apparent dismay as Hoad detonates his spectacularly horizontal serves.

Smith, in a remote part of the grounds, is slowly extinguishing Jaime Fillol. Tall, straightforward, All-American, Stan Smith is ranked number one in the United States. He grew up in Pasadena, where his father sold real estate. A fine basketball player,

Smith gave it up for tennis. He is a big hitter who thinks with caution. Under the umpire's chair is his wallet. The locker rooms of Wimbledon are only slightly less secure than the vaults of Zurich, but Smith always takes his wallet with him to the court. Fillol, a *Chileno*, supple and blue-eyed, says "Good shot" when Smith drives one by him. Such remarks are rare at Wimbledon, where Alphonse would have a difficult time finding Gaston. The players are not, for the most part, impolite, but they go about their business silently. When they show appreciation of another player's shot, it is genuine. There is no structure to Fillol's game. Now he dominates, now he crumbles. Always he faces the big, controlled, relentless power of the all-but-unwavering Smith. Smith does not like to play on these distant courts close to the walls of the Wimbledon compound. The wind rattles the ivy and the ivy sometimes rattles Smith—but hardly enough to save Fillol.

John Alexander has brown hair that shines from washing. It hangs straight and touches the collar of his shirt in a trimmed horizontal line. The wind gusts, and the hair flows behind him. Not yet twenty, he is tall, good-looking, has bright clear eyes, and could be a Shakespearean page. In his right hand is a Dunlop. He drives a forehand deep crosscourt. There is little time for him to get position before the ball comes back—fast, heavy, fizzing with topspin.

In Alexander's mind, there is no doubt that the man on the other side of the net is the best tennis player on earth. He hit with him once, in Sydney, when Laver needed someone to warm him up for a match with Newcombe. But that was all. He has never played against him before, and now, on the Number 1 Court, Alexander feels less the hopeless odds against him than a sense of being honored to be here at all, matched against Laver in the preeminent tournament of lawn tennis. The Number 1 Court is one of Wimbledon's two stadiums, and it is a separate closed world, where two players are watched in proximity by seven thousand pairs of eyes. Laver is even quicker and hits harder than Alexander had imagined, and Alexander, in his nervousness, is overhitting. He lunges, swings hard, and hits wide.

Laver is so far ahead that the match has long since become an

▲Hurlingham▶

exhibition. Nonetheless, he plays every point as if it were vital. He digs for gets. He sends up topspin lobs. He sprints and dives for Alexander's smashes. He punches volleys toward the corners and, when they miss, he winces. He is not playing against Alexander. He is playing against perfection. This year, unlike other years, he does not find himself scratching for form. He feels good in general and he feels good to be here. He would rather play at Wimbledon than anywhere else at all, because, as he explains, "It's what the atmosphere instills here. At Wimbledon things come to a pitch. The best grass. The best crowd. The royalty. You all of a sudden feel the whole thing is important. You play your best tennis."

Laver, playing Alexander in the second round, is in the process of defending the Wimbledon title. In the history of this sport, no player has built a record like Laver's. There have been only three grand slams—one by Budge, two by Laver. Wimbledon is the tournament the players most want to win. It is the annual world championship. Budge won Wimbledon twice. Perry won it three times. Tilden won it three times. Laver has won Wimbledon four times, and no one at Wimbledon this afternoon has much doubt that he is on his way to his fifth championship. There are one hundred and twenty-eight men in this tournament, and one hundred and twenty-seven of them are crowded into the shadow of this one small Australian. Winning is everything to tennis players, although more than ninety-nine per cent of them are certain losers—and they expect to lose to him. Laver, who has a narrow and delicate face, freckles, a hawk's nose, thinning red hair, and the forearm of a Dungeness crab, is known to all of them as Rocket. Alexander, who is also Australian and uses a Dunlop no doubt because Laver does, has just aced the Rocket twice and leads him 40–love. To prepare for this match, Alexander hit with Roger Taylor, who is left-handed, and practiced principally serving to Taylor's backhand. Alexander serves again, to Laver's backhand. When Laver is in trouble, fury comes into his game. He lashes out now and passes Alexander on the right. He passes Alexander on the left. He carries him backward from 40–love to advantage out. Alexander runs to the net under a big serve. A crosscourt backhand goes by him so fast that his racquet does not move. In the press section, Roy McKelvie, dean of English tennis writers, notifies all the other tennis writers that beating Laver would be a feat comparable to the running of the first four-minute mile. The match is over. "Thank you," Laver says to Alexander at the net. "I played well." A person who has won two grand slams and four Wimbledons can say that becomingly. The remark is honest and therefore graceful. Alexander took four games in three sets. "I've improved. I've learned more possibilities," he says afterward. "It should help me. The improvement won't show for a while, but it is there."

Roger Taylor leans against the guardrail on the sun-deck roof of the Players' Tea Room. He is twenty-five feet above the ground — the Players' Tea Room is raised on concrete stilts — and from that high perspective he can see almost all the lawns of Wimbledon. There are sixteen grass courts altogether, and those that are not attended with grandstands are separated by paved walkways ten feet wide. Benches line the edges of the walkways. Wimbledon is well designed. Twenty-five thousand people can move about in its confined spaces without feeling particularly crowded. Each court stands alone and the tennis can be watched at point-blank range. The whole compound is somehow ordered within ten acres and all paths eventually lead to the high front façade of the Centre Court, the name of which, like the name Wimbledon itself, is synecdochical. "Centre Court" refers not only to the *ne plus ultra* tennis lawn but also to the entire stadium that surrounds it. A three-story dodecagon, with a roof that shelters most of its seats, it resembles an Elizabethan theater. Its exterior walls are alive with ivy and in planter boxes on a balcony above its principal doorway are rows of pink and blue hydrangeas. Hydrangeas are the hallmark of Wimbledon. They are not only displayed on high but also appear in flower beds among the outer courts. In their pastel efflorescence, the hydrangeas appear to be geraniums that have escalated socially. When the Wimbledon fortnight begins each year, London newspapers are always full of purple language about the green velvet lawns and the pink and blue hydrangeas. The lawns are tough and hard and frequently somewhat brown. Their color means nothing to the players or to the ground staff, and this is one clue to the superiority of Wimbledon courts over the more lumpy but cosmetic sods of tennis lawns elsewhere. The hydrangeas, on the other hand, are strictly show business. They are purchased for the tournament.

Taylor is watching a festival of tennis from the roof of the tearoom. Szorenyi against Morozova, Roche against Ruffels, Brummer against O'Hara, Drysdale against Spear—he can see fourteen matches going on at the same time, and the cork-popping sound of the tennis balls fills the air. "This is the greatest tournament in the world," he says. "It is a tremendous thrill to play in it. You try to tune yourself up for it all year." Taylor is somewhat unusual among the people milling around him on the sun deck. For the most part, of course, they are aliens and their chatter is polyglot. Hungarians, Japanese, Finns, Colombians, Greeks—they come from forty nations, while home to Taylor is a three-room flat in Putney, just up the road from Wimbledon. Taylor is a heavy-set man with dark hair and a strong, quiet manner. His father is a Sheffield steelworker. His mother taught him his tennis. And now he is seeded sixteenth at Wimbledon. It took him five sets to get out of the first round, but that does not seem to have shaken his composure. His trouble would appear to be in front of him. In the pattern of the draw, the sixteenth seed is the nearest seeded player to the number-one seed, which is tantamount to saying that Taylor's outlook is pale.

On the promenade below, a Rolls-Royce moves slowly through the crowd. It contains Charlie Pasarell, making his appearance to compete in singles. Is Pasarell so staggeringly rich that he can afford to ride to his matches in a Rolls-Royce? Yes—as it happens—but the Rolls in this case is not his. It is Wimbledon's and it has been sent by the tennis club to fetch him. Wimbledon is uniquely considerate toward players, going to great lengths to treat them as if they were plenipotentiaries from their respective nations and not gifted gibbons, which is at times their status elsewhere. Wimbledon has a whole fleet of Rolls-Royces—and Mercedes, Humbers, and Austin Princesses—that deploys to all parts of London, to wherever the players happen to be staying, to collect them for their matches. Each car flies from its bonnet a small pennon in the colors of Wimbledon—mauve and green. Throughout the afternoons, these limousines enter the gates and murmur through the crowd to deliver to the locker rooms not only the Emersons, the Ashes, the Ralstons, and the Roches but also the Dowdeswelles, the Montrenauds, the Dibleys, and the Phillips-Moores.

In the Players' Tea Room, the players sit on pale-blue wicker chairs at pale-blue wicker tables eating strawberries in Devonshire cream. The tearoom is glassed-in on three sides, overlooking the courts. Hot meals are served there, to players only—a consideration absent in all other places where they play. Wimbledon is, among other things, the business convention of the tennis industry, and the tearoom is the site of a thousand deals—minor endorsements, major endorsements, commitments to tournaments over the coming year. The Players' Tea Room is the meat market of international tennis. Like bullfight impresarios converging on Madrid from all parts of Spain at the *Feria* of San Isidro, tournament directors from all parts of the world come to the Players' Tea Room at Wimbledon to bargain for—as they put it—"the horseflesh." The tearoom also has a first-rate bar, where, frequently enough, one may encounter a first-rate bookie. His name is Jeff Guntrip. He is a trim and modest-appearing man from Kent. His credentials go far deeper than the mere fact that he is everybody's favorite bookie. Years ago, Guntrip was a tennis player. He competed at Wimbledon.

In the Members' Enclosure, on the Members' Lawn, members and their guests are sitting under white parasols, consuming best-end-of-lamb salad and strawberries in Devonshire cream. Around them are pools of goldfish. The goldfish are rented from Harrods. The members are rented from the uppermost upper middle class. Wimbledon is the annual convention of this stratum of English society, starboard out, starboard home. The middle middle class must have its strawberries and cream, too, and—in just the way that hot dogs are sold at American sporting events—strawberries

At Hurlingham ▶

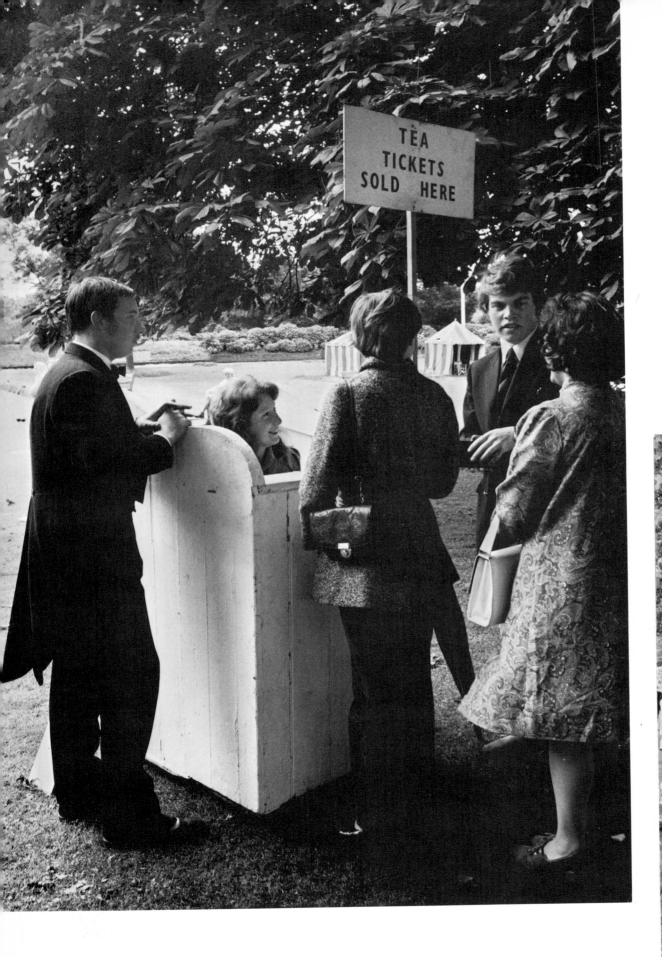

TEA
TICKETS
SOLD HERE

PRAMS AND KARICOTS
MAY NOT LEAVE
THE PATHS OR DRIVES
EXCEPT IN THE
CHILDREN'S TEA AREA.

Roche   Newcombe Davidson   Newcombe▶

Hewitt

Perry

Laver   van Dillen   Metreveli   Smith

Metreveli

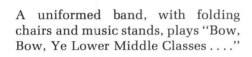

A uniformed band, with folding chairs and music stands, plays "Bow, Bow, Ye Lower Middle Classes...."

Froeling   Parun

Tinling

Borotra

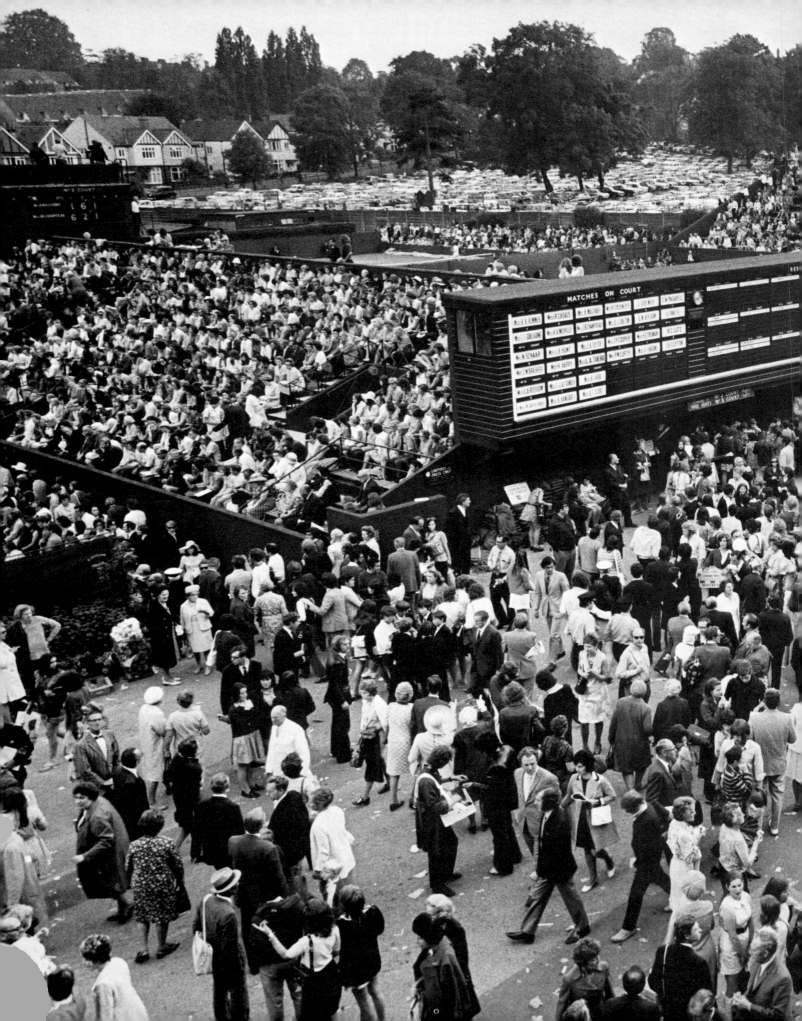

Sedgman

Okker   Laver

Sedgman

Laver

Davidson

Melville   Curtis

Chanfreau

Tiriac

Newcombe

Fillol

Emerson

Goolagong

Riessen

Ulrich

BARCLAYS BANK

NORTH HALL

ADJOINING STAIRCASE 14

INFORMAT

Women's Royal Voluntary Service

USED BALLS
will be **ON SALE**
OPPOSITE LEFT LUGGAGE OFFICE
after **3** P.M. *Price* £1·90 *PER DOZ.*

USED TICKETS
will be on Sale at the
**NORTH WEST
TICKET BOX**
NO SALES before 5·30 p.m.

RE-SALE *of* USED TICKETS
For
**NATIONAL
FIELDS ASSO**
Yesterday's Takings
TOTAL *Takings to date*

IN THE EVENT OF NO
PLAY, OR CURTAILMENT
OF PLAY, NO MONEY
PAID FOR RESERVED
SEATS OR FOR GROUND
ADMISSION AT THE
TURNSTILES CAN BE
REFUNDED

and thick Devonshire cream are sold for five shillings the dish from stalls on the Tea Lawn and in the Court Buffet. County representatives, whoever they are, eat strawberries and cream in the County Representatives' Enclosure. In the Officials' Buttery, officials, between matches, eat strawberries and cream. An occasional strawberry even makes its way into the players' locker rooms, while almost anything else except an authentic player would be squashed en route. The doors are guarded by bobbies eight feet tall with night sticks by Hillerich & Bradsby. The Ladies' Dressing Room at Wimbledon is so secure that only two men have ever entered it in the history of the tournament — a Frenchman and a blind masseur. The Frenchman was the great Jean Borotra, who in 1925 effected his entry into the women's locker room and subsequently lost his Wimbledon crown.

The Gentlemen's Dressing Room is *sui generis* in the sportive world, with five trainer-masseurs in full-time attendance. Around the periphery of the locker areas are half a dozen completely private tub rooms. When players come off the courts of Wimbledon, they take baths. Huge spigots deliver hot waterfalls into pond-size tubs, and on shelves beside the tubs are long-handled scrub brushes and sponges as big as footballs. The exhausted athletes dive in, lie on their backs, stare at the ceiling, and float with victory or marinate in defeat. The tubs are the one place in Wimbledon where they can get away from one another. When they are finally ready to arrange themselves for their return to society, they find on a shelf beneath a mirror a bottle of pomade called Extract of Honey and Flowers.

Smith comes into the locker room, slowly removes his whites, and retreats to the privacy of a tub closet, where, submerged for twenty-five minutes, he contemplates the loss of one set in the course of his match with Fillol. He concludes that his trouble was the rustling ivy. Scott comes in after a 14–12 finish in a straight-set victory over Krog. Scott opens his locker. Golf balls fall out. Scott runs four miles a day through the roughs of the golf course that is just across Church Road from the tennis club — The All-England Lawn Tennis and Croquet Club, Wimbledon. Other players — Graebner, Kalogeropoulos, Diepraam, Tiriac — are dressing for other matches. Upwards of sixty matches a day are played on the lawns of Wimbledon, from two in the afternoon until sundown. The sun in the English summer takes a long time going down. Play usually stops around eight p.m.

Leaving the locker room dressed for action, a tennis player goes in one of two directions. To the right, a wide portal with attending bobbies leads to the outer courts. To the left is a pair of frosted-glass doors that resemble the entry to an operating amphitheater in a teaching hospital. Players going through those doors often enough feel just as they would if they were being wheeled in on rolling tables. Beyond the frosted glass is the Centre Court—with the BBC, the Royal Box, and fourteen thousand live spectators in close propinquity to the hallowed patch of ground on which players have to hit their way through their nerves or fall if they cannot. There is an archway between the locker room and the glass doors, and over this arch the celebrated phrase of Kipling has been painted: "IF YOU CAN MEET WITH TRIUMPH AND DISASTER AND TREAT THOSE TWO IMPOSTORS JUST THE SAME."

Rosewall is on the Number 8 Court, anesthetizing Addison. Rosewall wears on his shirt the monogram BP. What is this for? Has he changed his name? Not precisely. Here in this most august of all the milieus of tennis, here in what was once the bastion of all that was noblest and most amateur in sport, Rosewall is representing British Petroleum. Rosewall represents the oil company so thoroughly, in fact, that on the buff blazer he wears to the grounds each day, the breast pocket is also monogrammed BP. There is nothing unusual in this respect about Rosewall. All the tennis players are walking billboards. They are extensions of the outdoor-advertising industry. Almost everything they drink, wear, and carry is an ad for some company. Laver won his grand slams with a Dunlop. He has used a Dunlop most of his life. His first job after he left his family's farm in Queensland was in a Dunlop factory in Sydney, making racquets. Recently, though, he has agreed to use Donnay racquets in certain parts of the world, and Chemold [gold-colored metal] racquets elsewhere, for an aggregate of about thirty thousand dollars a year. In the United States, he still uses his Dunlops. Donnay has him under contract at Wimbledon; however, the word among the players is that the Rocket is still using his Dunlops but has had them repainted to look like Donnays. Roche and Emerson are under contract to Chemold. They also have golden rackets. All things together, Ashe makes about one hundred and twenty-five thousand dollars a year through such deals. He gets fifty thousand dollars for using the Head Competition, the racquet that looks like a rug beater. He gets twenty-five thousand dollars from Coca-Cola for personal appearances arranged by the company and for drinking Coke in public as frequently as he can, particularly when photographers happen to be shooting him. Lutz and Smith are under contract to consume Pepsi-Cola—in like volume but for less pay. Ask Pasarell if he likes Adidas shoes. "I do, in Europe," he enthuses. He is paid to wear Adidas in Europe, but in the United States he has a different deal, the same one Lutz, Graebner, Smith, and King have, with Uniroyal Pro Keds.

Players endorse nets, gut, artificial court surfaces, and every item of clothing from the jock on out. Some players lately have begun to drink—under contract—a mysterious brown fluid called Biostrath Elixir. Made in a Swiss laboratory, it comes in small vials and contains honey, malt, orange juice, and the essences of ninety kinds of medicinal herbs. Others have signed contracts to wear copper bracelets that are said to counteract voodoo, rheumatism, and arthritis. Nearly everyone's clothing contract is with one or the other of the two giants of tennis haberdashery—Fred Perry and René Lacoste. When Pilic appears in a Perry shirt and Ashe in a Lacoste shirt, they are not so much wearing these garments as advertising them. Tennis is a closed world. Its wheeler-dealers are bygone players (Kramer, Dell). Its outstanding bookie is a former player. Even its tailors, apparently, must first qualify as Wimbledon champions—Lacoste, 1925, 1928; Perry, 1934, 1935, 1936. Rosewall has somehow escaped these two. He wears neither the alligator emblem of Lacoste nor the triumphal garland of Perry. However, he is hardly in his shirt for nothing. In addition to the BP, Rosewall's shirt displays a springing panther—symbol of Slazenger. All this heraldry makes him rich before he steps onto the court, but it doesn't seem to slow him up. He is the most graceful tennis player now playing the game, and gracefully he sutures Addison, two, four and zero.

The Russians advance in mixed doubles. Keldie and Miss Harris have taken a set from the Russians, but that is all the Russians will yield. Keldie is a devastatingly handsome tall fellow who wears tinted wrap-around glasses and has trouble returning serve. Miss Harris has no difficulty with returns. In mixed doubles, the men hit just as hard at the women as they do at each other. Miss Harris is blonde, with her part in the middle and pigtails of the type that suggests windmills and canals. She is quite pretty and her body is lissome all the way to her ankles, at which point she turns masculine in Adidas shoes with three black bands. The Russians show no expressions on their faces, which are young and attractive, dark-eyed. The Soviet Union decided to go in for tennis some years ago. A program was set up. Eight Russians are now at Wimbledon, and these—Metreveli and Miss Morozova—are the outstanding two. Both use Dunlops. They play with balletic grace—remarkable, or so it seems, in people to whose part of the world the sport is so alien. Miss Morozova, a severely beautiful young woman, has high cheekbones and almond eyes that suggest remote places to the east—Novosibirsk, Semipalatinsk. The Russians, like so many players from other odd parts of the earth, are camouflaged in their playing clothes. They are haberdashed by Fred Perry, so they appear more to come from Tennis than from Russia. Think how bad but how distinctive they would look if their clothes had come from GUM. Think what the Indians would look like, the Brazilians, the Peruvians, the Japanese, if they brought their clothes from home. Instead, they all go to Fred Perry's stock room on Vigo Street in London and load up for the year. The Russians are not permitted to take cash back to Russia, so they take clothing instead and sell it when they get home. Perry has a line of colored garments as well as white ones, and the Russians take all that is red. Not a red shirt remains in stock once the Russians have been to Vigo Street. Miss Morozova fluidly hits a backhand to Keldie's feet. He picks it up with a half volley. Metreveli puts it away. Game, set and match to Metreveli and Miss Morozova. No expression.

Graebner and Tiriac, on Court 3, is a vaudeville act. The draw has put it together. Graebner, the paper salesman from Upper Middle Manhattan, has recently changed his image. He has replaced his horn-rimmed glasses with contact lenses, and he has grown his soft and naturally undulant dark-brown hair to the point where he is no longer an exact replica of Clark Kent but is instead a living simulacrum of Prince Valiant. Tiriac hates Wimbledon. Tiriac, who is Rumanian, feels that he and his doubles partner, Nastase, are the best doubles team in the world. Wimbledon disagrees. Tiriac and Nastase are not seeded in doubles, and Tiriac is mad as hell. He hates Wimbledon and by extension he hates Graebner. So he is killing Graebner. He has taken a set from him, now leads him in the second, and Graebner is fighting for his life. Tiriac is of middle height. His legs are unprepossessing. He has a barrel chest. His body is encased in a rug of hair. Off court, he wears cargo-net shirts. His head is covered with medusan wires. Above his mouth is a mustache that somehow suggests that this man has been to places most people do not imagine exist. By turns, he glowers at the crowd, glares at the officials, glares at God in the sky. As he waits for Graebner to serve, he leans forward, swaying. It is the nature of Tiriac's posture that he bends forward all the time, so now he appears to be getting ready to dive into the ground. Graebner hits one of his big crunch serves, and Tiriac slams it back, down the line, so fast that Graebner cannot reach it. Graebner throws his racquet after the ball. Tiriac shrugs. All the merchants of Mesopotamia could not equal Tiriac's shrug. Graebner serves again. Tiriac returns, and stays on the base line. Graebner hits a backhand that lands on the chalk beside Tiriac. "Out!" shouts the linesman. Graebner drops his racquet, puts his hands on his hips, and examines the linesman with hatred. The linesman is seventy-two years old and has worked his way to Wimbledon through a lifetime of similar decisions in Somerset, Cornwall, and Kent. But if Graebner lives to be ninety, he will never forget that call, or that face. Tiriac watches, inscrutably.

Even in his Adidas shoes and his Fred Perry shirt, Tiriac does not in any way resemble a tennis player. He appears to be a panatela ad, a triple agent from Alexandria, a used-car salesman from central Marrakesh. The set intensifies. Eleven all. Twelve all. Graebner begins to chop the turf with his racket. Rain falls. "Nothing serious," says Mike Gibson, the referee. "Play on." Nothing is serious with Gibson until the balls float. Wimbledon sometimes has six or eight showers in an afternoon. This storm lasts one minute and twenty-two seconds. The sun comes out. Tiriac snaps a backhand past Graebner, down the line. "Goddamn it!" Graebner shouts at him. "You're so lucky! My God!" Tiriac has the air of a man who is about to close a deal in a back room behind a back room. But Graebner, with a Wagnerian forehand, sends him spinning. Graebner, whose power is as great as ever, has continually improved as a competitor in tight places. The forehands now come in chords. The set ends 14–12, Graebner; and Graebner is still alive at Wimbledon.

When the day is over and the Rolls-Royces move off toward central London, Graebner is not in one. Graebner and his attorney waive the privilege of the Wimbledon limousines. They have something of their own—a black Daimler, so long and impressive that it appears to stop for two traffic lights at once. Graebner's attorney is Scott, who is also his doubles partner. They have just polished Nowicki and Rybarczyk off the court, 6–3, 10–12, 6–3, 6–3, and the Daimler's chauffeur takes them the fifteen miles to the Westbury, a hotel in Mayfair that is heavy with tennis players. Emerson is there, and Ashe, Ralston, Pasarell, Smith, Lutz, van Dillen. Dell and Kramer are both there. Dell, lately captain of the American Davis Cup Team, has created a principality within the anarchy of tennis. He is the attorney-manager of Ashe, Lutz, Pasarell, Smith, Kodes, and others. Dell and Kramer sit up until three a.m. every night picking lint off the shoulders of chaos. Their sport has no head any more, no effective organization, and is still in the flux of transition from devious to straightforward professionalism. Kramer, who is, among other things, the most successful impresario the game has ever known, once had all the power in his pocket. Dell, who is only thirty-two, nightly tries to pick the pocket, although he knows the power is no longer there. Every so often they shout at each other. Kramer is an almost infinitely congenial man. He seems to enjoy Dell in the way that a big mother cat might regard the most aggressive of the litter—with nostalgic amusement and, now and again, a paw in the chops.

Ashe goes off to Trader Vic's for dinner dressed in a sunburst dashiki, and he takes with him two dates. Ralston joins them, and raises an eyebrow. "There is no conflict here," Ashe says, calmly spreading his hands toward the two women. Later in the evening, Ashe will have still another date, and she will go with him to a casino, where they will shoot craps and play blackjack until around one a.m., when Ashe will turn into a tennis player and hurry back to the hotel to get his sleep.

In his flat in Dolphin Square, Laver spends the evening, as he does most evenings, watching Western films on television. Many players take flats while they are in England, particularly if they are married. They prefer familial cooking to the tedium of room service. Some stay in boardinghouses. John Alexander and fifteen other Australians are in a boardinghouse in Putney. Dolphin Square is a vast block of flats, made of red brick, on the Embankment overlooking the Thames. Laver sits there in the evening in front of the television set, working the grips of his racquets. He wraps and rewraps the grips, trying for just the right feel in his hand. If the movie finishes and some commentator comes on and talks tennis, Laver turns him off and rotates the selector in quest of additional hoofbeats. He unwraps a new grip for the third or fourth time and begins to shave the handle with a kitchen knife. He wraps the grip again, feels it, moves the racket through the arc of a backhand, then unwraps the grip and shaves off a little more wood.

Gonzales sometimes drills extremely small holes in his racquets to change the weight. Gonzales, who is not always consistent in his approach to things, sometimes puts lead tape on his racquets to increase the weight. Beppe Merlo, the Italian tennis player, strings his own racquets, and if a string breaks while he is playing, he pulls gut out of his cover and repairs the damage right there on the court. Merlo likes to string his racquets at thirty pounds of tension—each string as tight as it would be if it were tied to a rafter and had a thirty-pound weight hanging on it. Since most players like their racquets at sixty pounds minimum, Merlo is extremely eccentric. He might as well be stringing snowshoes. When someone serves to him, the ball disappears into his racquet. Eventually, it comes out and it floats back toward his opponent like a milkweed seed. Merlo's game does not work at all well on grass. He is fantastic on clay.

Many players carry their own sets of gut with them. Professional stringers do the actual work, of course, using machines that measure the tension. Emerson likes his racquets at sixty-three pounds, very tight, and so does Smith. Since the frame weight of "medium" tennis racquets varies from thirteen to thirteen and three-quarters ounces, Smith goes to the Wilson factory whenever he can and weighs and feels racquets until he has selected a stack of them. He kills a racquet in six weeks. The thing doesn't break. It just becomes flaccid and dies. Strings go dead, too. They last anywhere from ten to twenty-eight days. Smith likes a huge grip—four and seven-eighths inches around. Some Americans wrap tape around their handles to build them up, and then they put new leather grips on. Australians generally like them smaller, four and five-eighths, four and a half. As Laver whittles away beside the television, he is progressing toward four and a half. When he is ready to go to bed, he switches off the television and, beside it, leaves a little pile of wood chips and sawdust on the floor.

Dennis Ralston carries his own pharmacy with him wherever he goes—Achromycin, Butazolidin, Oxazepam, Robaxin, Sodium Butabarbital. He is ready for anything, except sleep. The night before a match, he lies with a pillow over his head and fights total awareness. At three a.m., he complains bitterly about the traffic on New Bond Street outside the Westbury. There is no traffic on New Bond Street, outside the Westbury. Mayfair is tranquil in the dead of night, even if the tennis players are not. All over London, tennis players are staring open-eyed at dark ceilings. Some of them get up in the night and walk around talking to themselves—while Laver sleeps in Dolphin Square. Laver can sleep anywhere—in cars, trains, planes. He goes to bed around one a.m., and always sets an alarm clock or he would oversleep, even before a final.

Laver becomes quieter before a match. He and his wife, Mary, ordinarily laugh and joke and kid around a lot together, but he becomes silent as a match draws near. "The faster the pace, the more demands there are upon him, the better," she says. So Laver goes out in the morning and does the shopping. He drops off the laundry. Sometimes he washes clothes in the bathtub. He goes to his favorite butcher and buys a steak. He also buys eggs and greens. Back in the flat, two and a half hours before the match, he cooks his training meal. It is always the same—steak, eggs, and greens. He likes to cook, and prefers to do it himself. It keeps him busy. Then he gets into his car—a hired English Ford—and drives to Wimbledon. He ignores the club limousines. He wants to drive. "If he weren't a tennis player, he'd be a road racer," Mary says. "He has a quick, alert mind. He's fast. He's fast of body, and his mind works that way as well. The faster the pace of things, the faster he moves." He particularly likes driving on the left-hand side of the road. It reminds him of Australia, of which he sees very little any more. His home is in California. Each day, he plots a different route through Greater South London to Wimbledon. This is his private rally. It is a rule of the tournament that if a player is so much as ten minutes late, his opponent wins by a walkover. Laver knows his labyrinth—every route alternative, every mews and byway, between the Embankment and the tennis club, and all the traffic of London has yet to stop him. He turns off Church Road into the parking lot. His mind for many hours has been preoccupied with things other than tennis, with cowboys and sleep and shopping lists and cooking and driving. He never ponders a draw or thinks about an opponent. But now he is ready to concentrate his interest on the game—for example, on Wimbledon's opening day, when the defending champion starts the tournament with a match in the Centre Court.

Laver walks under the Kipling line and through the glass

doors, and fourteen thousand people stand up and applaud him, for he is the most emphatic and enduring champion who has ever played on this court. He stacks his extra racquets against the umpire's chair, where the tournament staff has placed bottles of orange squash and of Robinson's Lemon Barley Water should he or his opponent require them during change-overs. There is plain water as well, in a jug called the Bartlett Multipot. Behind the umpire's chair is a green refrigerator, where tennis balls are kept until they are put into play. A ball boy hands him two and Laver takes the court. He swings easily through the knockup. The umpire says, "Play." Laver lifts his right hand, sending the first ball up into the air, and the tournament is under way. He swings, hits. His opponent can barely touch the ball with his racquet. It is a near ace, an unplayable serve, 15–love. Laver's next serve scythes into the backhand court. It is also unplayable. 30–love.

The man across the net is extremely nervous. His name is George Seewagen. He comes from Bayside, New York. This is his first Wimbledon and his friends have told him that if you don't get a game in the first round, you never get invited back. Seewagen would like to get two games. At Forest Hills thirty-four years ago, Seewagen's father played J. Donald Budge in the opening round. The score was 6–0, 6–1, 6–0. When Seewagen, Jr., arrived in London, he was, like nearly everyone else, tense about the luck of the coming draw, and before it was published he told his doubles partner, "Watch me. I'll have to play Laver in the Centre Court in the first round." The odds were one hundred and eleven to one that this would not happen, but Seewagen had read the right tea leaf, as he soon learned.

"It was hard to believe. I sort of felt a little bit upset. Moneywise, London's pretty expensive. First-round losers get a hundred pounds and that's not much. I figured I needed to win at least one match in order to meet my expenses, but now I'd had it. Then I thought of the instant recognition. People would say, 'There's the guy that's opening up Wimbledon with Laver.' At least my name would become known. But then, on the other hand, I thought, What if I don't get a game? Think of it. What if I don't win even one game?"

Seewagen is an extremely slender—in fact, thin—young man with freckles, a toothy grin, tousled short hair. He could be Huckleberry Finn. He looks nineteen and is actually twenty-three. His credentials are that he played for Rice University, that he beat someone named Zan Guerry in the final of the 1969 amateur championship in Rochester, and that he is the varsity tennis coach at Columbia University. There were, in other words, grounds for his gnawing fears. By the eve of Wimbledon, Seewagen's appearance was gaunt.

Everyone goes to Hurlingham on that ultimate Sunday afternoon. All through the previous fortnight, the tennis players of the world have gradually come to London, and by tradition they first convene at Hurlingham. Hurlingham is a Victorian sporting club with floor-to-ceiling windows, sixteen chimney pots, and wide surrounding lawns—bowling lawns, tennis lawns, croquet lawns, putting lawns—under giant copper beeches, beside the Thames. Some players play informal sets of doubles. Others merely sit on the lawns, sip Pimm's Cups under the sun, and watch women in pastel dresses walking by on maroon pathways. In the background are people in their seventies, dressed in pure white, tapping croquet balls with deadly skill across textured grasses smooth as broadloom. A uniformed band, with folding chairs and music stands, plays "Bow, Bow, Ye Lower Middle Classes" while tea is served beneath the trees—a strawberry tart, sandwiches, petits fours, fruitcake, and a not-so-bitter macaroon. Arthur Ashe, eating his tea, drinking the atmosphere, says, "This is my idea of England." On a slope a short distance away, Graham Stillwell, Ashe's first-round opponent, sits with his wife and his five-year-old daughter, Tiffany. This is the second straight year that Ashe has drawn Stillwell in the first round at Wimbledon, and last year Stillwell had Ashe down and almost out—twice Stillwell was serving for the match—before Ashe won the fifth set, 12–10. Reporters from the *Daily Mirror* and the *Daily Sketch* now come up to Ashe and ask him if he has been contacted by certain people who plan to demonstrate against the South African players at Wimbledon. "Why should they contact me?" Ashe says. "I'm not a South African." Mrs. Stillwell rises from the sloping lawn and stretches her arms. "My God! She's pregnant again," Ashe observes. Jean Borotra, now seventy-two, is hitting beautiful ground strokes with Gardnar Mulloy. Borotra wears long white trousers. Two basset hounds walk by, leashed to a man in a shirt of broad pink and white stripes. The band is playing the music of Albéniz. The lady tennis players drift about, dressed, for some reason, in multicolored Victorian gowns. Laver, in dark slacks and a sport shirt of motley dark colors, stands near the clubhouse, watching it all with his arms folded. He seems uncomfortable. He looks incongruous—small, undynamic, unprepossessing, vulnerable— but every eye at Hurlingham, sooner or later in the afternoon, watches him in contemplation. He stands out no more than a single blade of grass, but no one fails to see him, least of all Seewagen, who stands at the edge of the party like a figure emerging from a haunted forest. He wears an old, worn-out pair of light-weight sneakers, of the type that tennis players do not use and sailors do, and a baggy gray sweater with the sleeves shoved far up his thin brown arms. Veins stand out on the backs of his hands and across his forearms. He grins a little, but his eyes are sober. His look is profoundly philosophical. Gene Scott informs him that players scheduled for the Centre Court are entitled to a special fifteen minutes of practice on an outside court beforehand. "Good, I'll take McManus," Seewagen says. McManus, from Berkeley and ranked tenth in the United States, is left-handed. He is also short and redheaded. He has the same build Laver has, much the same nose, and similar freckles as well. Players practicing with McManus easily fantasize that they are hitting with the Rocket himself, and thus they inflate their confidence. McManus is the favorite dummy of everyone who has to play against Laver. Ashe speaks quietly to Seewagen and tells him not to worry. "You'll never play better," Ashe says. "You'll get in there, in the Centre Court, and you'll get inspired, and then when the crowd roars for your first great shot, you'll want to run into the locker room and call it a day."

"I hope it isn't a wood shot," says Seewagen, looking straight ahead.

Game to Laver. He leads, one game to love, first set. Laver and

Seewagen change ends of the court. Laver went out to the Ponte-vecchio last night, on the Old Brompton Road. He ate lasagna and a steak *filet* with tomato sauce. He drank Australian beer. Then he went home and whittled a bit before retiring. At Chesham House, in Victoria, Seewagen fell asleep in his bed reading *Psycho Cybernetics*, by Maxwell Maltz. After one game, Seewagen has decided that Laver is even better than he thought he was. Laver is, for one thing, the fastest of all tennis players. He moves through more square yards per second than anyone else, covering ground like a sonic boom. In his tennis clothes, he is not unprepossessing. His legs are powerfully muscled. His left forearm looks as if it could bring down a tree. He is a great shotmaker, in part because he moves so well. He has every shot from everywhere. He can hurt his opponent from any position. He has extraordinary racquet-handling ability because his wrist is both strong and flexible. He can come over his backhand or slice it. He hits big shots, flick shots, spin shots, and rifle shots on the dead run. He lobs well. He serves well. His forehand is the best in tennis. He has one weakness. According to Gonzales, that is, Laver has one weakness— his bouncing overhead. The bouncing overhead is the shot a tennis player hits when a bad lob bounces at his feet and he cannon-balls his helpless opponent. Gonzales is saying that Laver has no weaknesses at all. Seewagen walks to the base line, visibly nervous, and prepares to serve. He is not pathetic. There is something tingling about a seven-hundred-to-one shot who merely shows up at the gate. In the end, at the net, Laver, shaking hands, will say to him gently, "You looked nervous. It's very difficult playing in here the first time over." Seewagen begins with a double fault. Love–15. Now, however, a deep atavistic athleticism rises in him and defeats his nerves. He serves, rushes, and punches two volleys past Laver, following them with an unplayable serve. 40–15. Serve, rush, volley—game to Mr. Seewagen. Games are one all, first set.

"His topspin is disguised," Seewagen notes, and he prepares, with a touch of unexpected confidence, for Laver's next service assault. Game to Mr. Laver. He leads, two games to one, first set. Seewagen now rises again, all the way to 40–15, from which level he is shoved back to deuce. Tossing up the ball, he cracks a serve past Laver that Laver can barely touch, let alone return. Advantage Seewagen. The source of all this power is not apparent, but it is coming from somewhere. He lifts the ball. He blasts. Service ace. Right through the corner. The crowd roars. It is Seewagen's first great shot. He looks at the scoreboard—two all—and it gives him what he will describe later as a charge. ("At that moment, I should have walked off.") 6–2, 6–0, 6–2.

Hewitt, in anger, hits one into the grandstand and it goes straight toward an elderly lady. She makes a stabbing catch with one hand and flips the ball to a ball boy. There is nothing lightweight about this English crowd. Ted Heath, Margaret, Anne, Charles, Lady Churchill, and the odd duke or baron might turn up—diverting attention to the Royal Box—but withal one gets the impression that there is a high percentage of people here who particularly know where they are and what they are looking at. They queue for hours for standing room in the Centre Court. They miss nothing and they are polite. The crowd at Forest Hills likes dramaturgy and emotion—players thanking God after chalk-line shots or falling to their knees in total despair—and the crowd in the Foro Italico throws cushions. But the British do not actually approve of that sort of thing, and when one of the rogue tennis players exhibits conduct they do not like, they cry, "Shame!"

"You bloody fools!" Hewitt shouts at them.

Hewitt has the temper of a grenade. He hits another ball in anger. This time it goes over the roof and out of sight. "Shame, Hewitt, shame!"

Rain falls. Umbrellas bloom. Mike Gibson's mustache is drooping from the wet, but he says, "It's not much. Play on." All matches continue. The umbrellas are black, red, green, yellow, orange, pink, paisley, and transparent. It is cold at Wimbledon. It often is—shirt sleeves one day, two pullovers and a mack the next. Now the players are leaving water tracks on the courts, and Gibson at last suspends play. Groundsmen take down the nets and cover the lawns with canvas. The standees do not give up their places, in the cold rain. The groundsmen go in under the grandstand to the Groundsmen's Bar, where they drink lager and offer one another cigarettes. "Will you have a smoke, Jack, or would you rather have the money?" The sun comes out for exactly three minutes. Then more rain falls. Half an hour later, play resumes.

Dell is supposed to be on Court 14, playing mixed doubles, but he is still in a phone booth talking to the office of Guntrip, the bookie. Dell bets heavily on his own players—one hundred pounds here, two hundred there—and even more heavily against Laver. Dell is a talented gambler, and he views the odds as attractive. Besides, Dell and Laver are the same age, and Dell can remember beating Laver when they were boys. Shrewd and realistic, Dell reasons that anyone who ever lost to Donald Dell cannot be invincible. In the end, he repeats his name to the clerk at Guntrip's, to be sure the clerk has it right. "Dell," he says. "D as in David, E as in Edward, L as in loser, L as in loser."

The field of women players is so thin that even some of the women themselves are complaining. Chubby little girls with orange ribbons in their hair hit parabolic ground strokes back and forth and seem incongruous on courts adjacent to an Emerson, a Lutz, or a Pasarell, whose ground strokes sound like gunfire. Billie Jean King slaps a serve into the net and cries out, "That stinks!" Billie Jean is trimmer, lighter, more feminine than she was in earlier years, and somehow less convincing as a challenger to Margaret Court. Yet everyone else seems far below these two. Miss Goolagong is still some distance away. "Have you seen the abo, Jack?" says Robert Twynam, head groundsman, to his assistant, John Yardley. The interesting new players are the ones the groundsmen find interesting. They go to watch Miss Goolagong and they notice that her forehand has a tendency to go up and then keep going up. When it starts coming down, they predict, she will be ready for anybody, for her general game is smooth and quite strong and unflinchingly Australian. Australians never give up, and this one is an aborigine, a striking figure with orange-brown hair and orange-brown skin, in a Teddy Tinling dress and Adidas shoes, with a Dunlop in her hand. Margaret Court is breaking everything but the cool reserve of Helga Niessen, the Berlin model.

Between points, Miss Niessen stands with her feet crossed at the ankles. The ankles are observed by a Chinese medical student who is working the tournament with the ground staff. "Look at those ankles. Look at those legs," he says. "She is a woman." He diverts his attention to Margaret Court, who is five feet eight, has big strong hands and, most notably, the ripple-muscled legs of a runner. "Look at those legs," says the Chinese medical student. "The lady is a man."

Hoad, in the Centre Court, is moving so slowly that a serve bounces toward him and hits him in the chest. The server is El Shafei, the chocolate-eyed Egyptian. Hoad is in here because all Britain wants to see him on television. Stiffened by time and injury, he loses two sets before his cartilage begins to bend. In the third set, his power comes, and he breaks the Egyptian. The Egyptian is a heavy-framed man, like Hoad, and in the fourth set, they pound each other, drive for drive—wild bulls of the tennis court. Hoad thinks he is getting bad calls and enormous anger is rising within him. The score is three all. Shafei is serving, at deuce. He lifts the ball and blows one past Hoad for a service ace. Hoad looks toward the net-cord judge with expanding disbelief. He looks toward Shafei, who has not moved from the position from which he hit the serve—indicating to Hoad that Shafei expected to hit a second one. Slowly, Hoad walks forward, toward the officials, toward Shafei, toward the center of the court. The crowd is silent. Hoad speaks. A microphone in Scotland could pick up what he says. "That goddamned ball was a let!" The net-cord judge is impassive. The umpire says, "May I remind you that play is continuous." Hoad replies, repeats, "That goddamned ball was a let!" He turns to the Egyptian. Unstirring silence is still the response of the crowd, for one does not throw hammers back at Thor. "The serve was a let. You know that. Did you hear it hit the tape?" Hoad asks, and Shafei says, "No." Hoad lifts his right arm, extends it full length, and points steadily at the Egyptian's eyes. "You lie!" he says slowly, delivering each syllable to the roof. A gulf of quiet follows and Hoad does not lower his arm. He draws a breath slowly, then says again, even more slowly, "You lie." Only Gar-

Sedgman

Maud

Dibley

Gonzales

Nastase

Duke and Duchess of Kent

Gorman

Kramer

Laver

Emerson   Smith

Wade   Howe

King   Davidson

Battrick

Centre Court►

Fillol

Graebner

rick, possibly Burton, could have played that one. It must have stirred bones in the Abbey, and deep in the churchyards of Wimbledon, for duels of great moment here have reached levels more serious than sport. This is where Canning fought Castlereagh, where Pitt fought Tierney, where Lord Winchelsea fought the Duke of Wellington. Ceawlin of the West Saxons fought Ethelbert of Kent here, when the terrain was known as Wibbas dune—home of the Saxon, Wibba (Wibbas dune, Wipandune, Wilbaldowne, Wymblyton). Hoad returns to the base line, and when the Egyptian serves again, Hoad breaks him into pieces. Game and fourth set to Hoad. Sets are two all. In his effort, though, Hoad has given up the last of his power. Time has defeated him. Twice the champion, he has failed his comeback. His energy drains away in the fifth set—his last, in all likelihood, at Wimbledon.

Ralston, at the umpire's chair, pries the cap off a vial of Biostrath and sucks out the essences of the ninety medicinal herbs. Dennis has no contract with Biostrath. He is not drinking the stuff for money. He is drinking it for his life. Beside him stands his opponent, John Newcombe, the second-best forehand, the second-best volley, the second-best tennis player in the world. Dennis follows the elixir with a Pepsi-Cola, also without benefit of a contract. The score is 4–5, first set. Ralston and Newcombe return to the base lines, and Ralston tosses up a ball to serve. The crowd is chattering, gurgling like a mountain stream. Prince Charles has just come in and is settling into his seat. "Quiet, please," says the umpire, and the stream subsides. Ralston serves, wins—six all. Seven all. Eight all. Nine all. Ten all. There is a lot of grinning back and forth across the net. Newcombe drives a backhand down the line. Ralston leaps, intercepts it, and drops the ball into Newcombe's court for a winner. Newcombe looks at Ralston. Ralston grins. Newcombe smiles back. It is an attractive match, between two complete professionals. Newcombe passes Ralston with a forehand down the line. "Yep," says Ralston. Ralston finds a winner in a drop shot overhead. "Good shot," calls Newcombe. Eleven all. When they shout, it is at themselves. Newcombe moves to the net behind a fragile approach shot, runs back under a humiliatingly good lob, and drives an off-balance forehand into the net. "John!" he calls out. "Idiotic!" Ralston tosses a ball up to serve, but catches it instead of hitting it. He is having a problem with the sun, and he pauses to apologize to Newcombe for the inconvenience the delay might be causing him. Small wonder they can't beat each other. Grace of this kind has not always been a characteristic of Ralston—of Newcombe, yes, but Ralston grew up tightly strung in California, and in his youth his tantrums were a matter of national report. He is twenty-seven now and has changed. Quiet, serious, introspective, coach of the United States Davis Cup Team, he has become a professional beyond the imagination of most people who only knew him long ago. He plans his matches almost on a drawing board. Last night, he spent hours studying a chart he has made of every shot Newcombe has hit in this tournament. 13–12. Dennis opens another Biostrath and another Pepsi-Cola. He knows what the odds have become. The winner of this set, since it has gone so far, will in all likelihood be the winner of the match. Ralston has been a finalist at Wimbledon. But he has never won a major international tournament. In such tournaments, curiously enough, he has played Newcombe ten times and has won seven, but never for the biggest prize. Newcombe has a faculty for going all the way. Ralston, meanwhile, has pointed his life toward doing so at least once, and, who knows, he tells himself, this could be the time. He toes the line and tosses up the ball. He catches it, and tosses it up again. The serve is bad. The return is a winner. Love–15. He has more trouble with the sun. Love–30. Catastrophe is falling from nowhere. Love–40. Serve, return, volley. 15–40. He serves. Fault. He serves again. Double fault. Game and first set to Newcombe, 14–12. Ralston looks up, over the trigger of a thousand old explosions, and he forces a smile. 14–12, 9–7, 6–2. When it is over, the ball boys carry out seven empty bottles of Pepsi-Cola and four empty vials of the ninety medicinal herbs.

Kramer is in a glassed-in booth at one corner of the court, commenting on the action for the BBC. For an American to be engaged to broadcast to the English, extraordinary credentials, of one kind or another, are required. Just after the Second World War, Kramer first displayed his. Upwards of fifty American players now come to Wimbledon annually, but Kramer, in 1946, was one of three to cross the ocean. "Now it's a sort of funsy, 'insy' thing to do," he has said. "But in my time, if you didn't think you had a top-notch chance, you didn't come over. To make big money out of tennis, you had to have the Wimbledon title as part of your credits. I sold my car, a 1941 Chevrolet, so I could afford to bring my wife, Gloria, with me." That was long before the era of the Perry-Lacoste-Adidas bazaar, and Kramer, at Wimbledon, wore his own clothes — shorts that he bought at Simpson's and T shirts that had been issued to him during the war, when he was a sailor in the United States Coast Guard. Now, as he watches the players before him and predicts in his expert way how one or the other will come slowly unstuck, he looks past them across the court and up behind the Royal Box into an entire segment of the stadium that was gone when he first played here. At some point between 1939 and 1945, a bomb hit the All-England tennis club, and with just a little more wind drift it would have landed in the center of the Centre Court. Instead, it hit the roof over the North East Entrance Hall. Kramer remembers looking up from the base line, ready to serve, into a background of avalanched rubble and twisted girders against the sky. He slept in the Rembrandt, which he remembers as "an old hotel in South Kensington," and he ate steak that he had brought with him from the United States, thirty pounds or so of whole tenderloins. Needless to say, there was no Rolls-Royce flying Wimbledon colors to pick him up at the Rembrandt. Kramer went to Wimbledon, with nearly everyone else, on the underground — Gloucester Road, Earl's Court, Fulham Broadway, Parsons Green, Putney Bridge, East Putney, Southfields, Wimbledon. He lost the first time over. A year later, he returned with his friend Tom Brown and together they hit their way down opposite sides of the draw and into the Wimbledon final. A few hours before the match, Kramer took what remained of his current supply of *filet mignon*, cut it in half, and shared it with Tom Brown. Kramer was twenty-five and his game had come to full size — the Big Game, as it was called, the serve, the rush, the jugular volley. When Kramer proved what he could do, at Wimbledon, he changed for all fore-seeable time the patterns of the game. He destroyed Brown in forty-seven minutes, still the fastest final in Wimbledon's history, and then—slender, crewcut, big in the ears—he was led to the Royal Box for a word or two with the King and Queen. The Queen said to him, "Whatever happened to that redheaded young man?" And Kramer told her that Donald Budge was alive and doing O.K. The King handed Kramer the Wimbledon trophy. "Did the court play well?" the King asked him. "Yes, it did, sir," Kramer answered. It was a tennis player's question. In 1926, the King himself had competed in this same tournament and had played in the Centre Court. A faraway smile rests on Kramer's face as he remembers all this. "Me in my T shirt," he says, with a slight shake of his head.

Frew McMillan, on Court 2, wears a golfer's billowing white visored cap, and he looks very much like a golfer in his style of play, for he swings with both hands and when he completes a stroke his arms follow the racquet across one shoulder and his eyes seem to be squinting down a fairway. Court 2 has grandstands on either side and they are packed with people. McMillan is a low-handicap tennis player who can dig some incredible ground strokes out of the rough. A ball comes up on his right side and he drives it whistling down the line, with a fading hook on the end. The ball comes back on his left side and, still with both hands, overlapping grip, he hits a crosscourt controlled-slice return for a winner. The gallery applauds voluminously. McMillan volleys with two hands. The only strokes he hits with one hand are the serve and the overhead. He has an excellent chip shot and a lofty topspin wedge. He putts well. He is a lithe, dark, attractive, quiet South African. In the South African Open, he played Laver in the final. Before Laver had quite figured out what sort of a match it was, McMillan had him down one set to nought. Then Laver got out his mashie and that was the end of McMillan in the South African Open. When McMillan arrived in London and saw the Wimbledon draw, he felt, in his words, a cruel blow, because his name and Laver's were in the same pocket of the draw, and almost inevitably they would play in the third round. "But maybe I have a better chance against him earlier than later," he finally decided. "You feel you have a chance. You have to—even if it is a hundred to one." Now the grandstands are jammed in Court 2 and, high above, the railing is crowded on the Tea Room roof, for McMillan, after losing the first set, has broken Laver and leads him 5-3 in the second.

"I got the feeling during the match that I had more of a chance beating him on the court than thinking about it beforehand. You realize the chap isn't infallible. It's almost as if I detected a chip in his armor."

Laver has netted many shots and has hit countless others wide or deep. He cannot find the lines. He is preoccupied with his serves, which are not under control. He spins one in too close to the center of the service box. McMillan blasts it back. Advantage McMillan. Laver lifts the ball to serve again. Fault. He serves again. Double fault. Game and set to McMillan, 6-3.

When this sort of thing happens, Laver's opponent seldom lives to tell the tale. One consistent pattern in all the compiled scores in his long record is that when someone takes a set from him, the score of the next set is 6-0, Laver, or something very near it. Affronted, he strikes twice as hard. "He has the physical strength to hit his way through nervousness," McMillan says. "That's why I believe he's a great player."

Laver breaks McMillan in the opening game of the third set. He breaks him again in the third game. His volleys hit the corners. His drives hit the lines. McMillan's most powerful blasts come back at him faster than they left his racquet. McMillan hits a perfect drop shot. Laver is on it like the light. He snaps it unreachably down the line. Advantage Laver. McMillan hits one deep to Laver's backhand corner, and Laver, diving as he hits it, falls. McMillan sends the ball to the opposite corner. Laver gets up and sprints down the base line. He not only gets to the ball—with a running forehand rifle shot, he puts it away. It is not long before he is shaking McMillan's hand at the net. "Well played," McMillan says to him (6-2, 3-6, 6-0, 6-2). "Yes, I thought I played pretty well," Laver tells him. And they make their way together through the milling crowd. McMillan will frequently say what a gentle and modest man he finds Laver to be. "It may be why he is what he is," McMillan suggests. "You can see it in his eyes."

B.M.L. de Roy van Zuydewijn is a loser in the Veterans' Event—gentlemen's doubles. So is the seventy-two-year-old Borotra. Riggs and Drobny, on Court 5, persevere. Over the years, Riggs and Drobny have eaten well. Each is twice the shadow of his former self. The Hungarians Bujtor and Stolpa are concentrating on Riggs as the weaker of the two.

Game to Seewagen and Miss Overton, the honey-blonde Miss Overton. They lead Dell and Miss Johnson five games to four, second set. Dell is not exactly crumbling under the strain. These peripheral matches are fairly informal. Players talk to one another or to their friends on the side lines, catching up on the news. Seewagen and Miss Overton appear to be playing more than tennis. Dell is tired—up half the night making deals and arguing with Kramer, up early in the morning to do business over breakfast with bewildered Europeans, who find him in his hotel room in a Turkish-towel robe, stringy-haired and wan, a deceptive glaze in his eyes, offering them contracts written on flypaper.

The Russians enter the Centre Court to play mixed doubles. Princess Anne is in the Royal Box. The Russians hesitate, and look at each other in their ceramic way, and then they grin, they shrug, and they turn toward the Royal Box and bend their heads. The people applaud.

Nastase is Nijinsky—leaping, flying, hitting jump-shot overheads, sweeping forehands down the line. Tiriac is in deep disgrace. Together they have proved their point. They have outlasted most of the seeded pairs in the gentlemen's doubles. But now they are faltering against Rosewall and Stolle, largely because Tiriac is playing badly. Stolle hits an overhead. Tiriac tries to intercept it near the ground. He smothers it into the court. Nastase, behind him, could have put the ball away after it had bounced. Tiriac covers his face with one hand and rubs his eyes. He slinks back to the base line like someone caught red-handed. But now he redeems himself. The four players close in for a twelve-shot volley, while the ball never touches the ground. It is Tiriac who hits number twelve, picking it off at the hip and firing it back through Stolle.

Lutz crashes and the injury appears to be serious. Playing doubles in the Centre Court with his partner, Smith, he chases an angled overhead and he crashes into the low wall at the front of the grandstands. He makes no effort to get up. He quivers. He is unconscious. "Get a doctor, please," says the umpire. A nurse, in a white cap and a gray uniform that nearly reaches her ankles, hurries across the lawn. The crowd roars with laughter. There is something wondrous in the English sense of humor that surfaces in the presence of accidents, particularly if they appear to be fatal. The laughter revives Lutz. He comes to, gets up, returns to the court, shakes his head a few times, resumes play, and drives a put-away into the corner after an eight-shot ricochet volley. Lutz is tough. He was a high-school football player in California, and he once promised himself that he would quit tennis and concentrate on football unless he should happen to win the national junior championship. He won, and gave up football. Additional medical aid comes from outside the stadium. Another nurse has appeared. She hovers on the edge of play. When she sees an opportunity, she hurries up to Smith and gives him an aspirin.

If Lutz had broken three ribs, he would not have mentioned it as long as he continued to play, and in this respect he is like the Australians. There is an Australian code on the matter of injuries and it is one of the things that gives the Australians a stature that is not widely shared by the hypochondriac Americans and the broken-wing set from mainland Europe. The Australian code is that you do not talk about injuries, you hide them. If you are injured, you stay out, and if you play, you are not injured. The Australians feel contempt for players who put their best injury forward. An Australian will say of such a man, "I have never beaten him when he was healthy." Laver developed a bad wrist a year or so ago, at Wimbledon, and he and his wife together got into a telephone kiosk so that she could tape the wrist in secrecy. If he had taped it himself, no one would ever have known the story.

His wife would rather praise him than waltz with the Australian code. His wife is an American.

"Bad luck, Roger." This is what Roger Taylor's friends are saying to him, because he has to play Laver, in the fourth round, in the Centre Court tomorrow. The champion always plays in one of the two stadiums or on the Number 2 Court, the only places that can take in all the people who want to see him. "Don't worry, though, Roger. It's no disgrace if Rocket is the man who puts you out. You've got nothing to lose."

"I've got everything to lose," Taylor tells them. "To lose at Wimbledon is to lose. This is what competition is all about. You've got to think you have a chance. You might hope for twenty-five let cords or something, but you always think there's a chance you'll get through."

"Bad luck, Roger."

Roger takes a deep hot bath, goes home to his two-bedroom flat on Putney Hill, and continues to work himself up, talking to his mother, his father, and his wife, over a glass of beer.

"That's enough beer, Roger."

"I don't live like a monk. I want to loosen up." He eats a slice of fried liver and opens another beer. "All my chances will hinge on how well I serve. I'll have to serve well to him, to keep him a little off balance on his returns. If I can't do that, I'll be in dire trouble. If you hit the ball a million miles an hour, he hits it back harder. You can't beat a player like that with sheer speed—unless he's looking the other way. I plan to float back as many service returns as I can. The idea is not to let it get on top of you that you're going to play these people. There's a tendency to sort of lie down and roll over."

Games are three all, first set. Taylor feels weak from tension. Laver is at ease. "We'd played often enough," Laver will say later. "I knew his game—left-handed, slice serve, better forehand than backhand, a good lob. He's very strong. He moves well for a big man. There was no special excitement. My heart wasn't pounding quite as hard as it sometimes does."

Taylor floats back a service return, according to plan. Laver reaches high, hits a semi-overhead volley, and the ball lands in the exact corner of the court. It bounces into the stadium wall. The crowd roars for him, but he is also hitting bad shots. There is a lack of finish on his game. He wins the first set, 6–4.

"My concentration lapsed continually. I was aware of too many things—the troublesome wind, the court being dry and powdery. I magnified the conditions. I played scratchy in the first set. I felt I'd get better in the next set."

A break point rises against Laver in the first game of the second set. He lifts the ball to serve. He hits it into the net. "Fault." He spins the next one—into the net. "Double fault." "Oh, just throw it up and hit it," he says aloud to himself, thumping his fist into the strings of his racquet.

"When you lose your rhythm, serving, it's because of lack of concentration. I found myself thinking too much where the ball should be going. You don't think about your serve, you think about your first volley. If you think about getting your serve in, you make errors. I didn't know where my volleys were going. I missed easy smashes."

Taylor is floating back his returns. He is keeping Laver off balance. With his ground strokes, he is hitting through the wind. There is an explosion of applause for him when he wins the second set, 6–4. No one imagines that he will do more, but it is enough that Taylor, like McMillan, has won a set from Laver— and more than enough that he is English.

"Roger was playing some good tennis. When I played fairly well, he played better."

First game, third set—love–40—Laver serving. There is chatter in the crowd, the sound of the mountain stream. "Quiet, please!" Laver hits his way back to 30–40. He serves, rushes, and punches a volley down the line—out. Game and another service break to Taylor. Five times, Laver has hit his running rifle-shot forehand into the net. He has repeatedly double-faulted. His dinks fall short. His volleys jump the base line. Taylor, meanwhile, is hitting with touch and power. He is digging for everything. Laver is not covering the court. Both feet off the ground, Laver tries a desperation shot from the hip and he nets it. Advantage Taylor. Taylor serves — a near ace, unplayable. Game and third set to Taylor, 6–2. He leads two sets to one. Unbelievable. Now the time has certainly come for Laver to react, as he so often does, with vengeance.

"When your confidence is drained, you tend to do desperation shots. My desperation shots, a lot of times, turn matches. I felt something was gone. I didn't have strength to get to the net quickly. I can't explain what it was. If you're not confident, you have no weight on the ball. You chase the ball. You look like a cat on a hot tin roof."

Laver serves, moves up, and flips the volley over the base line. "Get it down!" he shouts to himself. His next volley goes over the base line. Now he double-faults. Now he moves under a high, soft return. He punches it into a corner. Taylor moves to the ball and sends it back, crosscourt. Laver, running, hits a rolling topspin backhand — over the base line. Advantage Taylor. Break point. The whispering of the crowd has become the buzz of scandal.

His red hair blowing in the wind, Laver lifts the ball to serve against the break. Suddenly, he looks as fragile as he did at Hurlingham and the incongruity is gone. The spectators on whom this moment is making the deepest impression are the other tennis players — forty or so in the grandstands, dozens more by the television in the Players' Tea Room. Something in them is coming free. The man is believable. He is vulnerable. He has never looked more human. He is not invincible.

"The serve is so much of the game. If you serve well, you play well. If not, you are vulnerable. If you play against someone who is capable of hitting the ball as hard as Roger can, you are looking up the barrel."

Laver serves. "Fault." He serves again. "Double fault." Game and service break to Taylor, fourth set. Laver, without apparent emotion, moves into the corner, and the shadow that until moments ago seemed to reach in a hundred directions now follows him alone. The standard he has set may be all but induplicable, but he himself has returned to earth. He will remain the best, and he will go on beating the others. The epic difference will be that, from now on, they will think that they can beat him.

Taylor lobs. Laver runs back, gets under the bouncing ball, kneels, and drives it into the net. He is now down 1–5. He is serving. He wins three points, but then he volleys into the net, again he volleys into the net, and again he volleys into the net—deuce. He serves. He moves forward. He volleys into the net. Advantage Taylor—match point. The sound of the crowd is cruel. "Quiet, please!" the umpire says. Laver serves, into the net. He appears to be trembling. He serves again. The ball does not touch the ground until it is out of the court beyond the base line.

Photographers swarm around him and around Taylor. "Well done, Roger. Nice," Laver says, shaking Taylor's hand. His eyes are dry. He walks patiently through the photographers, toward the glass doors. In the locker room, he draws a cover over his racquet and gently sets it down. On the cover are the words ROD LAVER—GRAND SLAM.

"I feel a little sad at having lost. I played well early in the tournament. I felt good, but I guess deep down something wasn't driving me hard enough. When I had somewhere to aim my hope, I always played better. Deep down in, you wonder, 'How many times do you have to win it?'"

TWYNAM
OF WIMBLEDON

A weed—in the vernacular of groundsmen in England—is
known as a volunteer, and there are no volunteers in the Centre
Court at Wimbledon. Robert Twynam, who grows the grass there,
is willing to accept a bet from anyone who is foolhardy enough to
doubt this. Twynam's lawn—nine hundred and thirty square
yards, one-fifth of an acre—is the best of its kind, and Twynam
has such affection for it that he spends a great deal of time just
looking at it. He takes long, compact walks on the Centre Court.
At times, he gets down on his hands and knees and crawls on it,
to observe the frequently changing relationships among the various plants there. Twynam keeps a diary for the Centre Court
("February 4: very sunny spells, Centre Court fine," "February 5:
cooler, little sun, Centre Court O.K."), and, in the words of one
member of Wimbledon's Committee of Management, "Mr. Twynam regards each blade of grass as an individual, with its own
needs, its own destiny, and its own right to grow on this blessed
piece of lawn." Twynam has been at Wimbledon almost fifty
years. Nearly all the greatest stars of tennis have played under his
scrutiny, and—while he knows a great deal about the game—his
appraisals of all of them seem to have been formed from the point

Twynam

Outside the Members' Enclosure

of view of the grass. "When Emmo puts his foot down . . ." Twynam will say, in reference to Roy Emerson, of Australia, "when Emmo puts his foot down, he is stepping on forty or fifty plants."

Working alone on his hands and knees somewhere between the base lines, Twynam raises one hand and affectionately slaps the surface of the lawn, which is so firm that an echo, like the sound of a rifle, returns from the roof of the grandstands. It is the third week of June, and the Wimbledon championships will begin in a few days. "This court brings the best out of the players," he comments. "They can make the ball speak, here on this court. The ball sometimes comes through so fast it sizzles. We've had some terrific battles here." The lawns of Wimbledon are his in more than a professional sense, for his own home is within the tennis club's compound, and tennis lawns are around it on three sides. His house has casement windows and a steep slate roof. Red roses grow up its walls. Twynam, his wife, and their children are the only people who live within the boundaries of the All-England grounds. At the edge of the grass of the Centre Court is a Lightfoot Automatic Electric Refrigerator, in which—for consistency of bounce and other, more subtle, reasons—tennis balls are chilled up to the moment that they are put into play. The Twynams kept their butter and milk in the refrigerator in the Centre Court until recently, when they bought a fridge of their own.

When Twynam describes tennis players, he is less likely to call them touch players or power players than to call them toe-draggers, sliders, or choppers. A right-handed toe-dragger will inscribe a semicircle in the lawn, with his right toe, as he serves; and by the end of a long match these crescent ruts can be so deep and distinct that they almost seem to have been burned into the ground. "They dig their toes. They drag their toes," Twynam says. "Once they get underneath the surface, away they go. Nothing will hold it." Understandably, Twynam prefers to see non-toe-draggers defeat toe-draggers in Wimbledon championships, but things do not always work out that way. The pre-eminent toe-draggers of this century have been Jean Borotra, Robert Falkenburg, and Jaroslav Drobny, each of whom won the Men's Singles Championship. Borotra won it twice. "Borotra was the worst ever,"

Twynam says. "He used to cut the court to pieces, he did. He dragged his toe something shocking. He was so awkward on his feet. He used to dig up the turf with his heavy great shoes and make shocking big holes. The Bounding Basque they used to call him. He slid a lot, too, as you can imagine." A slider runs to get into position, then slides a yard or so before executing a shot. "Of course that's what gets on the old court, you know," Twynam goes on. "They all slide to a certain extent, but the *great* players don't slide much. I mean, they know where the ball is coming, don't they? These foreign players do a lot of sliding. Czechs. French. Austrians as a rule are heavy-footed, too. One or two Americans used to slide. Falkenburg was a slider. He was one of our worst enemies all around. But Emmo never slides. Rosewall never slides. Don Budge never slid. Kramer never slid. Budge Patty—a gentleman player, he was. He played beautiful tennis. He never slid. He never dragged his toe. He was a genteel player, a nice player. He beat Frank Sedgman for the championship in 1950." A chopper, after losing a point, temporarily uses his racquet as an ax. There have been so many choppers at Wimbledon that Twynam sees no point in drawing up a list. The effect of the chopping is almost always the same—a depression in the lawn five inches long and an inch deep. When this happens, or when a slider takes a serious divot, play is interrupted while Twynam goes onto the court to repair the damage. He fills holes with a mixture of clay and grass cuttings; and when he replaces divots, he applies fresh clay, then a cupful of water, then the divot itself, which he sutures into place with matchsticks while the crowd and the competitors look on—an operation that usually takes three minutes.

Throughout the Wimbledon championships (known to the Wimbledon staff as The Fortnight), Twynam is close to the Centre Court and is prepared to go into action. He sits on a folding chair in the passage—between the Royal Box and the West Open Stand—that the players use to get from the clubhouse to the court. He places the chair very carefully beside the sloping wall of the grandstand, at the point where he can be as close as possible to the court without allowing his head to protrude into the view of the spectators, or paying customers, as he prefers to call them. Since he is five feet five inches tall, he can get quite close. From time to time, he nips into his house for a cup of tea or something to eat, where he continues to watch the Centre Court, on BBC television. On the salt shaker he uses are the words "Say little and think much." If anything goes wrong on the court, it is only a half-minute walk through his garden and past the Court Buffet, past the Wimpy hamburger kiosk, and into the stadium. The appearance he makes as he moves into the view of the crowds is arresting. He looks like a Member of Parliament. His hair is handsomely groomed, wavy, and silver gray. His mustache is sincere and reassuring, being just halfway between a handlebar and a pencil-line. His face, which has strong and attractively proportioned features, is weathered and tanned. He is trim and in excellent condition—nine stone five. He wears a gray suit, suede shoes, a white shirt, a regimental tie.

Twynam is not a horticulturist or a botanist or a herbarian, and his approach to the growing and care of his grass goes some distance beyond science. He is a praying man, and at least part of the time he is praying for the grass. One June, three days before The Fortnight began, he left all sixteen of Wimbledon's lawn-tennis courts uncovered, for he wanted to take advantage of what he believed would be a brief but soaking rain. Imprudently, he did not even get out his tarpaulins against the possibility of a heavier storm. After the rain had been falling steadily for ninety minutes, he began to worry. The courts could absorb only two hours of rain and still be in perfect condition for the opening matches. "If it had gone longer, I would have been in serious trouble," he said afterward. "I got down on me knees and prayed, I did. I got down on me knees and prayed." The rain stopped almost precisely two hours after it had begun, and the lawns were in perfect condition on opening day. Some nights, out of consideration for others, he prays that it will rain, but not until ten-thirty—"when everyone's gone home from the boozer," he explains. "A drop of rain, no more—just to give it a drink, just to cool the grass." The Wimbledon lawns are top-dressed from time to time with miscellaneous loams, and the new soil is eventually pressed into the old with rollers. When asked if the courts are periodically checked to see that they are level, Twynam says, "Oh, no, bloody fear. We haven't got the time. We trust in the good Lord. They're pretty good for level, considering they get such a banging about." Only once every five or six years is the earth of Wimbledon tested for its pH factor. At last count, it was between 5 and 6—slightly acid.

In a drawer of a small chest in Twynam's sitting room are copies of important texts in his field, such as R.B. Dawson's *Lawns* and I.G. Lewis's *Turf.* Twynam has his personal pantheon of great figures in grass. The late William Coleman, one of his predecessors as Head Groundsman at Wimbledon, trained him and remains to this day something of a hero to Twynam, but not on the level of Sir R. George Stapledon, of whom Twynam speaks with obvious reverence ("He went into this lawn culture in a big way, you know"), and whose name is apparently the greatest one in the annals of English turf. It was Stapledon who developed the superior modern strains of English grasses. There is a passage in *Turf* in which I.G. Lewis writes, "At a seaside town on the west coast of Wales the first steps towards better grasses for this country were taken by a man in whom profound belief mingled with immense vision—a combination which in all ages has been recognized as the precursor of genius. Aberystwyth was the seaside place and R. George Stapledon the man. With the results of a wide survey of grassland in this country uppermost in his mind he set out, as others of his native Devon had set out centuries before, on a journey of discovery. Stapledon, however, sought new grasses, not new lands." These books in Twynam's drawer are used more as talismans than as references. Twynam does not use them in his season-to-season work. Some years ago, he regularly read a journal called *Turf for Sport,* but found it so redundant he gave it up. He does have a look, now and again, at the *Groundsman,* but his way with his lawns is not so much planned or studied as it is felt. He has his experience, his sense of the weather, and a crew of twelve, and

Barthes

Sedgman

Laver

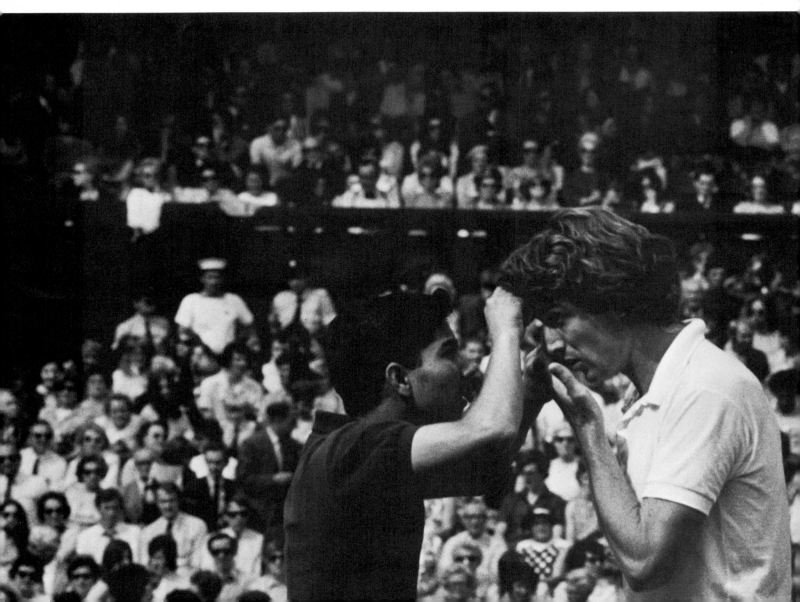

Gorman

Court

Ulrich

Ballboy and Barthes

Ralston

Ashe   Rosewall   Stolle

DOGS

Dogs must be kept on Leads on
Saturdays. Sundays & Public Holidays
Between 12 noon and 6·30 p.m.
from 1ST MAY to 30TH SEPTEMBER.
By Order of the Committee.

Melville

Mr. and Mrs. Pinto Bravo

Pigeon

Ticket queues

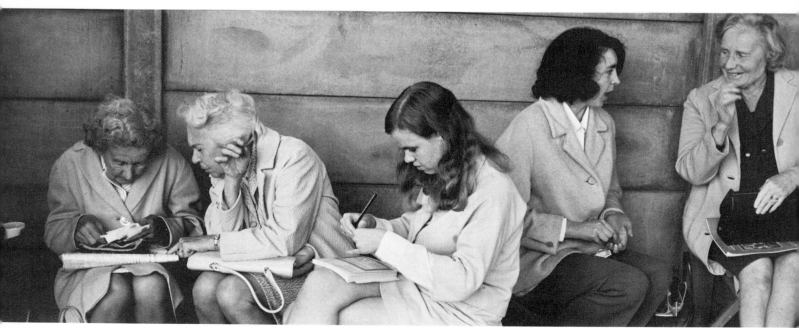

Gorman

Gonzales

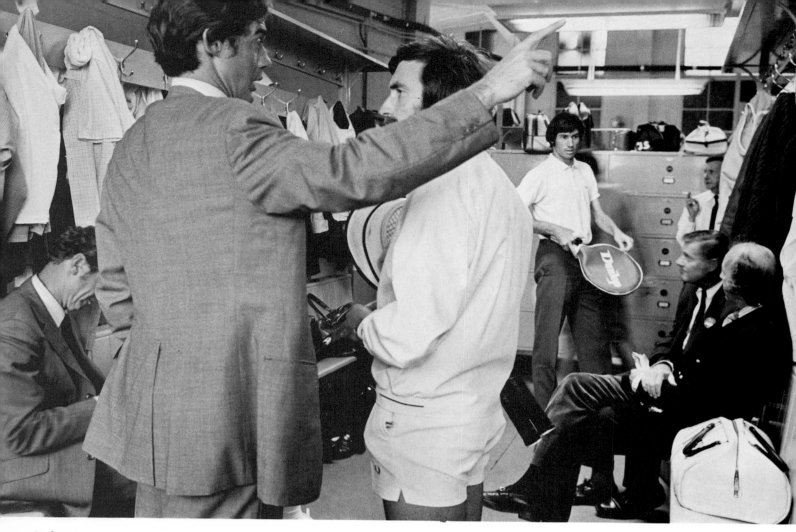

Sedgman   Scott   Matthews   Froeling   Schroeder   Collins

Hogan   Tuero

Mr. and Mrs. Dell

Dibley

Dell   Kodes   Goolagong

The Players' Tea Room is the meat market of international tennis.

Simpson   Spear   Case   Di Matteo

Graebner

his lawns are acknowledged by tennis players from everywhere as the best in England and the best in the world.

The men in Twynam's crew, for the most part, are middle-aged and even elderly. Around all of them there is an atmosphere of individuality suggesting that no pressure or persuasion could cause them to wear white monkey-suit uniforms or soft rubber shoes, and they don't. Players are forbidden to go on the courts in anything but flat-soled tennis shoes, but the men of Twynam's crew walk around on the lawns all day in street shoes with sharp-edged leather heels. Typically, they work in their shirtsleeves, with the cuffs turned halfway up their forearms, and now and again they hitch up their braces as they mow or roll the lawns. Most of them have been at Wimbledon for decades, but they appear to have been pulled in off the street for an afternoon's work. For thirty-seven years, it was Twynam himself who lined out the courts ("If the lines are dead straight and the corners are true, it's a picture; it's not everyone can line a court out — to get it really spot on"), but he has turned over this responsibility to John Yardley, a tall sharp-featured man with a good eye and a steady hand.

Twynam likes to point out that two standard rules of lawn care are "Do not use a heavy roller" and "Do not roll too often." "These rules are always broken at Wimbledon," he says. According to *Turf,* "Occasional rolling with a light roller is permissible, but very heavy rolling packs the surface and prevents healthy root growth." A similar warning appears in *Lawns,* which goes on to say, "For spring use the roller seldom need be heavier than 2 cwt." Twynam and his crew use something ten times heavier than that. They call it the Old Horse Roller. In season, they use it every day, and it weighs two thousand five hundred pounds. They drag it around by hand. No power machines of any kind are used on the Centre Court, and only for certain brief autumnal procedures are power machines used elsewhere at Wimbledon. The Old Horse Roller is equipped with shafts, in which a horse, its hooves padded, was once harnessed, but the horse was phased out long ago and now John Yardley gets between the shafts and four other men drag or shove the roller to help him. They heave like galley slaves.

The work is hard. Fights occasionally break out. One day the Old Horse Roller was reversing direction, slightly overlapping its previous path, when one old man got his feet tangled up in the feet of the man next to him. The second man, whose age was about sixty, raised a fist, loudly called the first man a bleeding bastard, then hit him hard, knocking his hat off. The first man, who appeared to be at least seventy-five, hit back. Yardley turned in the shafts and bawled them out. They calmed down, the hat was retrieved, and the Old Horse Roller began to move again. By mid-June, the turf of Wimbledon is packed down so firmly that the daily rolling has little effect. "What the roller does is put a polish on," Twynam said. "The court is firm enough as it is, but the roller makes a nice gloss on the top of the grass."

The lawns are mowed every day in the springtime — with hand mowers, of course. Power mowers frog and rib the courts — "frog" and "rib" being terms for various unkempt results — and, moreover, power mowers cannot be as finely adjusted as hand mowers. The height of the grass at Wimbledon is three-sixteenths of an inch. The mower that keeps it at that level is a sixteen-inch Ransome Certes, which has a high-speed, precision-ground, ten-knife cylinder, makes a hundred cuts every thirty-six inches, costs forty-one pounds twelve and six, and hums with the high sound of a vacuum cleaner while it moves. It throws its cuttings forward into a hooded catching device, the design of which causes the over-all machine to look very much like an infant's perambulator and the crewman who pushes it to look like a grandfather in St. James's Park. In the early spring, the courts are cut diagonally. In mid-spring, they are cut from side to side; and as The Fortnight approaches, the cuts are made the long way, end to end. Cutting the long way, the lawnmower is always pushed in the exact swaths that were cut the day before, and it always moves on each alternating swath in the same direction that was followed in earlier cuttings. The effect of this, to an observer at one end of the court, is that the lawn appears to be made of an enormous bolt of green seersucker, the alternating stripes being light and dark. If, in making the cut, the mower was going away from the observer's point of view, the cut appears light. If the mower was moving in the observer's direction, the cut appears dark. The light cuts and dark cuts have no influence on the bounce of the ball, but they follow the line of play and thus remind the players of the direction in which the ball is supposed to be hit.

"Grass grows at night, you know," Twynam says. "With a little warm rain, you can practically hear it growing." He puts his hand on the court. "Feel that. This hasn't been mowed for a day. Feel that little wisp on it." If the weather is warm and humid, the grass will grow as much as an eighth of an inch overnight, but it usually grows much less than that, and the tips that the mower shaves off the grass are often so small that Twynam refers to the aggregate as dust. Sometimes, after the Centre Court has been completely mowed, the removed cuttings can be held in the palms of two hands.

Somewhere in almost any English newspaper story of an opening day at Wimbledon, a poetic reference is made to the appearance of the lawn itself. "The turf was green velvet," said the *Times*. This gratifies Twynam less than one might imagine, for green velvet is the last thing he is trying to grow, and an edge comes into his voice when he describes groundsmen who develop their lawns for cosmetic effect. "These lawns at Wimbledon are not made to look at but to play on," he says—and as long as the lawns are alive and healthy he doesn't care what color they are, including brown. "Other courts are greener than these," Twynam goes on. "This is hard-growing, natural green. There's no nitrogen or phosphates or sulphate of ammonia forcing this green up. Grass that is forced up may look greener, but it is weaker and softer. Overfeed grass and you're not making good base grass. All you're doing is mowing. If you force-feed it, it gets all pappy and there's no guts in it. If you don't give it *any* fertilizer, you're asking for trouble, but don't give it much. One ounce per square yard. Grass doesn't want forcing. Let it grow hard. Leave the grass to struggle for itself. The deepest roots only go down about two and a half inches anyway. If we were to fertilize just before The Fortnight, use a seven-hundredweight roller once a week, and mow to a quarter of an inch, we'd have lovely green beautiful lawns. But we haven't fertilized these courts for three months. These are not ornamental lawns. This is a true hard surface for lawn tennis. This is hard-growing grass. And as soon as it grows, we go down and cut it off. These lawns are not here to be looked at. The world championship is played here." Whatever the reasons, the lawns of other front-line English tennis clubs—Roehampton, Queens, Hurlingham, Beckenham—do not have quite the same texture as the lawns of Wimbledon. Billie Jean King, of California, who has won three Ladies' Singles Championships at Wimbledon, says that the other English courts she has played on "are not half as good" as Wimbledon's. "The bounce varies in the other places," she explains. "One time the ball may skid, another time it may stand and float. But not at Wimbledon."

In Australia, grass courts are very good, and most players, Mrs. King included, say that the Australian surfaces are almost as good as Wimbledon's. Roy Emerson, who won Wimbledon in 1964 and 1965, goes further than that. He thinks that the center courts at Brisbane, Sydney, and Adelaide are the peers of the Wimbledon lawns. "The turf is good in Calcutta, too," Emerson says. "Wimbledon, Adelaide, Brisbane, Sydney, and Calcutta—that's the story on good grass courts throughout the world. Other than that, grass courts are pretty bad. Forest Hills is nowhere near it—very bad." Emerson's reverence for Wimbledon may have been reduced slightly in 1966, when, defending his title, he sprinted after a stop volley and—by Twynam's description—"got his racquet tied up in his pigeon toes, bowled over once, and finished up in a ball under the umpire's chair, tangled up in the microphone cables." In the accident, Emerson injured his shoulder, and as a result he lost the match and the chance to win Wimbledon three years in a row. "Wimbledon is fast and hard," Emerson says now, "but Wimbledon is sometimes a little slippery. The first couple of rounds, the courts are a bit green. There is still a lot of juice in the grass. In Australia, there is a bit more heat. The grass is hardier and isn't as slippery."

"I've seen football players hurt worse than that—with their ankles hanging by the cleats—get up and score goals!" Twynam says, remembering Emerson's accident. "It was a shame, that—when Emmo fell. Emmo is as pigeon-toed as a coot, like Frank Sedgman, but he usually has good footwork. He gets the feel of the lawn straightaway. He likes a court really fast. He likes the ball to come through. He's very quick. Emmo is a real machine. And he never makes a mess of a lawn. If Emmo sees a place kicked up, he goes out of his way and treads it back."

Developing a reasonably good tennis lawn in England is not the difficult feat that it is in, say, the United States. The English atmosphere, with its unextreme temperatures and its soft, reliable rains, makes the English land a natural seedbed for grass. At Cambridge, typically, there is a meadow behind St. John's College, on the west bank of the Cam, where cattle graze during much of the year, and where crocuses come shooting through by the thousand in March. Each year, the crocuses are mowed down, the grass is cut short, the cattle are driven to other meadows, posts and nets are erected, courts are lined out, and all kinds of dons, by-fellows, and undergraduates play tennis there. In another part of Cambridge, beside the university gymnasium, is a patch of lawn that basketball players ride their bicycles across all winter long on their way to and from the gym. In the spring, the same lawn is sometimes used for exhibition tennis matches on an important scale. Some years ago, when Vic Seixas was preparing to defend his Wimbledon championship, he played an exhibition match against Tony Trabert on the lawn beside the Cambridge gym. In England, grasses riot on the earth, obviously enough, but what happens after that—the ultimate quality of the playing surface—is a matter of the groundsman's style. Seixas, who was still competing at Wimbledon when he was forty-three, describes the Wimbledon turf as "cement with fuzz on it." Seixas lives in Villanova, Pennsylvania, and plays at the Merion Cricket Club, near his home. He says that the grass courts at Merion—and at Forest Hills and other American tennis clubs—are soft. "We don't have a proper conception of what grass should be," he goes on. "In American clubs, hard-working ground crews produce nice-looking lawns, but that's all they are—nice-looking. The turf has to be hard for the ball to bounce. In our country, the ball just dies. It's like playing it on a cushion. And in the soft ground you get holes and bad bounces. A bad grass court favors a weaker player and makes luck more important than skill. The Wimbledon people obviously feel that it's a very integral part of the game that the ball bounce properly. Surfaces cannot get much faster than at Wimbledon. The smoother the surface, the more the ball will shoot off it. Remember, though, the problems are greater in our country. I can't make grass grow in my own lawn."

For many years, before they were given their present house at Wimbledon, Twynam and his family lived in a small maisonette flat on the Kingston By-Pass, in Surrey. His back garden, which was sixteen feet wide and twenty feet long, was turfed with "a bit of old rough grass," which he mowed with no especial fidelity, since he cared nothing about its botanical origins or its earthly destiny. He has always concentrated on Wimbledon. He was born within a mile of the Centre Court. His father was a construction foreman from Connemara, who had crossed to England at the age of eighteen, and while still a very young man had attempted to emigrate to the United States. For obscure reasons, he was kept at Ellis Island for a number of weeks and then sent back to Britain. "I wouldn't have let him in, either," Twynam says. "He was the biggest bloody rogue that ever set foot in this country." When Twynam was two, his father left home and did not permanently return. Twynam was the youngest of six children. He went to school until he was fourteen and then tried working as a messenger for the General Post Office. He wore a pillbox hat and a black mackintosh, and he went around Chelsea and Battersea in all weathers on a red bicycle. He hated the hat, the coat, Chelsea, Battersea, the bicycle, and the weather, so he applied for a job as a ball boy at Wimbledon. The All-England Lawn Tennis and Croquet Club had full-time, resident ball boys when Twynam joined the staff—a luxury that the club gave up many years ago. Dressed in the club's green and mauve colors, Twynam spent three years retrieving faulted serves and put-aways, and then he was promoted to the ground crew.

"I ball-boyed for Vincent Richards, Jean Borotra, Henri Cochet, Bill Tilden, Sidney Wood, Alice Marble, Helen Wills Moody," he said one June evening, while he was enjoying a walk on the Centre Court. "Wills Moody was playing here when I first came, in the final, here on the Centre Court. Light and dainty, she was. I've never seen a woman take a divot. Alice Marble was tall, blond, strong, and manly — but no damage. Like Althea Gibson — a bit manly and not all that interesting to watch. Suzanne Lenglen was light, like a bloody ballet dancer, and never disturbed the courts at all. Helen Jacobs was a bit heavy-footed, but not bad. Mrs. Susman — Mrs. J.R. Susman — was the only 'worst enemy' we've ever had among the women. She used to drag her toe terrible when she served — terrible mess — oh, shocking. She used to scuff and slide. Slide on her right heel, drag her left toe. Always sliding she was, Susman. Women play tennis now like men did years ago, but they seldom hurt the grass. Billie Jean is light on her feet for a big girl. Maria Bueno is so light — a very dainty thing, she is."

The evening was quiet, in the extended twilight of the late spring, and the walk was long and helical. As Twynam moved around the court, he stopped from time to time — for no apparent reason — to stare at the turf in the way that some people stare into a log fire. In one of these moments, he said that he himself had once played in the Centre Court — but only briefly, and over forty years ago, with another groundsman. "It was just a knockup," he said, "but it was an odd experience, really. You seem like a lonely soul, stuck out here on your own in the vast arena." He opened a packet of cork-tipped Player's Weights and lighted one. During the Second World War, he said, he was a Leading Aircraftsman in the Royal Air Force, and he spent four years in control towers, "talking in" planes. In Poona, in the State of Bombay, to defeat boredom during a rest period, he organized a group that cleared an area in a grove of mango trees and built a red-clay tennis court. Until

1955 or so, he played tennis forty-five minutes a day, with other groundsmen, at Wimbledon, never sliding—or so he says—and never dragging his toe. The Wimbledon ground staff has its own tournament, and it has always been a professional tournament, for the winner receives, in addition to a fine silver trophy, a merchandise voucher that is convertible into goods in London stores. The competition is therefore without nonsense. Ball boys are used, and, as Twynam describes it, "We have a chap in the chair taking the umpire duty. There are base-line judges. The players wear flannels, slippers—no pure whites. Some wear a bloody collar and tie." Year after year, in the nineteen-thirties and nineteen-forties, Twynam got into the final, but he always lacked whatever it is that draws a player together in a championship final and gives him the thrust to win. But 1952, the year of Frank Sedgman, was also the year of Bob Twynam. In the ground-staff final, he defeated William Collis, and won his only Wimbledon championship. "I had quite a decent game in those days," he said. "But now I'm retired a bit. My game is going down." About a dozen times a season, he plays with his son, Robert—almost always on one of Wimbledon's ten hard-surface courts, where the ball bounces higher than on turf and the action is slower. "Yes, these grass courts are too much for me now," he admitted. "I watch the ball go by."

Each year, the opening match of the Wimbledon championships is traditionally played between the men's defending champion and some unfortunate and usually obscure fellow whose name happens to be paired with the champion's in the draw. The match is little more than ceremonial—no test for either the champion or the court. In 1966, for example, Emerson, the defender, was paired with one H.E. Fauquier, of Canada, and Emmo defeated him 6–0, 6–1, 6–2. In 1967, the defending champion was Manuel Santana, of Spain, and the player that came up opposite Santana in the draw was Charles Pasarell, an undergraduate at UCLA. Because Pasarell happened to be an American, his role as the customary opening-day sacrifice was an ironic extension of the humbled status of American men at Wimbledon, for men's tennis in the United States was in such a state of decline then that for the first time in thirty-nine years no American player was seeded in the Men's Singles Championship. All this only moderately interested Twynam. "That should be a good match," he said, "because the court will be in A-1 condition."

The draw was published during Overseas Week, as the Wimbledon staff refers to the seven days immediately preceding the tournament. During Overseas Week, tennis players from about fifty nations come to Wimbledon, unstrap their enormous stacks of rackets, and have at each other from eleven in the morning until deep in the evening, trying to effect ultimate refinements in their styles before the meeting that is regarded by all of them as the world-championship event in the sport. They practice—usually two-on-one—on the courts outside the stadium. No one ever practices on the Centre Court. Twynam walks around among them, watching the lawns and the weather. Given the imminence of The Fortnight, Overseas Week is a surprisingly relaxed and easygoing time, full of chatter and casual gossip. The players all know each other as if they had spent the past ten years in the same small boarding school, and, in a sense, they have. "They love these courts. They would sleep on them if you let them," Twynam says. "They love to come to Wimbledon. If they can't make it, it breaks their hearts. They come back with their children. The atmosphere is so beautiful here." In the air were the scent of roses and fresh-cut grass and the sound of tennis balls like the sound of popping corks. An Australian on Court 9 hit two drives into the tape at the top of the net. "You hit the ball over the net and into the court," he said to himself. "That's page 1, line 1." An American girl on Court 8 shouted at herself, "What's the story with my backhand?" English players kept calling "Sorry" to one another. "Sorry." Twynam saw a girl beside one court with oranges in her hand. "South African," he said. "If she's got oranges in her hand, she's a South African." Santana, practicing with Vic Seixas and Charlie Pasarell, drilled one past Pasarell at the net. "You're out of your mind," said Pasarell. Santana grinned toothily. Other remarks were flying around in Dutch and Danish, German and Polish, Serbo-Croatian. Twynam wandered off to one corner of the grounds and onto the croquet lawn. He said that on Sunday afternoons elderly members play croquet, two at a time. They wear all white, like the tennis players. Twynam tapped the croquet lawn with one foot, and said, "Make a nice nursery for the tennis lawns, wouldn't it, this?" Looking back across the courts, he said, "They're all first-class tennis players here. There are no rabbits here. We don't do this for love, you know. There's no jiggery-pokery. Nothing's too much trouble to cater to the players. They have medical services, masseurs, doctors, free rides to London. They can have anything they want, as long as they're playing tennis. They've got to play good tennis. We must take care of paying customers, not just friends who come in and look around and pay nothing. These players come here to play tennis. Even the second-rate players play good tennis here. This Wimbledon is not run for love. We English want the money, you know. We're a tight nation, we are. Any penny that's going, we'll have it." He paused a moment and then said he was going to have a look at the Centre Court. In the stadium, he made a close inspection of the turf. He pressed his fingers down on the dense, elastic surface. "Feel the fiber," he said. He withdrew his hand, and the turf sprang back. "The court is as alive as the players are," he went on. "There is an inch of fiber between the surface and the topsoil. Claw it. Claw it. See? There's something there to wear." About two feet down, he said, are the tops of tile land drains, set in a herringbone pattern in the local clay. Ten inches of clinker is above the drains, and over that is an inch of fine ash. Above the ash is ten inches of light and loamy topsoil, and in the topsoil are the roots of the lawn. When the surface of the lawn is looked at from a distance of inches, the differences among the various grasses there become pronounced. Some areas were lighter in shade than the grasses around them and were noticeably tinged with gray, in contrast to the flaring shamrock green of their neighbors. "The light patches are *Poa pratensis*," Twynam said. "Smooth-stalked meadow grass. The gray color is seed heads. One must mow close to get them. By rights, we don't want smooth-stalked meadow grass any more.

The greener patches are Chewings fescue and American brown-top—better pedigrees than the *Poa pratensis* now. The smooth-stalked meadow grass is coarse and doesn't make as good a mat as the fescue and the browntop. But it's been here for years. It's self-sowing—and it comes up in these pale-gray patches. We'll phase it out before long. You get a better game of tennis on the brown-top and the fescue. The fescue comes up into a tuft, and we mow it right down to the basal level. That forces the grass prostrate and makes it mat. The American browntop is shallow-rooted but hard-wearing. Americans have done a lot for lawns, you know. It's all Americanized. This browntop is actually what they call Oregon browntop. If you were a keen lawnmaker yourself, you'd use these strains. But you don't get a first-class lawn in two or three years. It takes twenty or thirty years to get a real lawn down. There's also a bit of creeping bent in here, but that's about all. One or two bas-tard grasses come in, like a bit of rough-stalked meadow grass, a bit of rye grass, a little bit of Yorkshire fog. They blow over, you see. But we pick them out. Yorkshire fog is bloody awful. Prickly. Spiky. Hairy. . . . Volunteers? Parsley piert, plantain, and pearl-wort are about all you get in here. We don't let them stay. . . . The only hard thing about this job is, you can't change your court over. The court is static. All the courts are static. We can't move them up or back or sideways. The lines are always in the same places and have been for forty-six years. Same toepieces. Same base lines. Same no man's lands. Same run-ups in the service areas. We get the same problems in the same places every year. In the autumn, on the other courts, we put in new turf—pieces one foot square from our own nursery—along the base lines and the run-ups. The Centre Court base lines and run-ups are almost always resown. The last time we turfed in here was six years ago. We oversow the rest of the court with seed, after pruning the roots with a hand fork and letting in some air and light. This year, we'll be using eighty per cent Dutch Highlight Chewings fescue and twenty per cent Oregon browntop. Then we give it a light top-dressing with a heavy loam, then a light roll, and it's ready to start germination— we hope. In November, we solid-tine the turf with potato forks, making deep holes two inches apart. Then we top-dress it again, with a ton of medium-to-heavy loam. Luting, it's called. The new soil is spread with a lute, a rake that has no tines. Extra-thick top dressing makes a firmer surface. The soil falls into the legs made by the potato fork. We never hollow-tine here—just a matter of opinion. The top-dressing soil comes from the Guildford area, here in Surrey, and it's a decent bit of stuff. Mow the grass once or twice in late autumn and it stays a half inch high until spring. You like a good winter, to lift up the roots. A good winter is a cold winter, what they call an open winter. It lifts the roots up and aerates them. The Centre Court is the hardest one to keep in good shape. It is shaded from the sun. Frost stays longer in here. There is less freedom of air. But in the spring we get a good top growth. It's called a good braird." He plucked a bit of browntop, or common bent grass, out of the turf and turned it slowly in his hand, describing its flat, hairless, spear-shaped leaves, its short rhizomes and stolons, its notched, blunt-topped ligules. Hunting around awhile, brushing past whole colonies of the predominant grasses, he finally came up with a plant he was seeking, its blades like stiff bristles, infolded and bluntly keeled, its ligules blunt, and its auricles rounded like shoulders. "There you are," he said. "A bit of creeping red fescue."

On Saturday afternoon, forty-eight hours before the championships began, four women members of the club—Mrs. C.F.O. Lister, Mrs. W.H.I. Gordon, Mrs. P.E. King, and Mrs. N.M. Glover—played on the Centre Court for an hour and twenty minutes so that Twynam, with this light rehearsal, could sense the timbre of the lawn. While the ladies—in pure white, of course—made light but competent movements around the court, driving long ground strokes at one another, Twynam said that a similar ritual occurs every year. "It gets the court knocked in a bit," he explained. "I watch them to see how the ball really does come up, you see. Then, if necessary, we can get the surface padded down a bit. It's coming through quite well, considering the wet we had yesterday. I've been looking for bad bounds, but there have been none. No trouble at all. It's coming through quite good."

That night, the court was covered. Twynam and his crew have an enormous tarpaulin — eight thousand sixty square feet. Winches at either end of the court raise the canvas, between spars, until it is high above the grass, looking like a vast pup tent. Air can circulate inside. Mildew won't form beneath the tent, as it will, sometimes, under a flat tarp. The crew can get the tent up in fourteen minutes. If rain comes during a match, they just drag it over the lawn, flat. Sunday morning, they removed it, then mowed, rolled, and marked the lawn. The white lines, put down with a forty-year-old machine, are made of pulverized chalk, called whiting. Lime is never used. It would burn the grass. The court was covered again at noon. At seven-thirty a.m. on Monday, the opening day, the court was uncovered. It was mowed again, rolled again, and — although it hardly appeared to need it — marked again.

The gates of the grounds were opened, and the crowds came in. Fourteen thousand five hundred people came into the Centre Court. Twynam looked them over. "From grocers' boys to kings we get here," he said. The sky was a mixture of clouds and blue. "The court is all right," Twynam said. "The court's O.K. We gave it a half hour's slow roll longways this morning, that's all. It could have had a little more rolling, but the players will pat it down, I hope." He set his chair in his accustomed spot, adjusting it so that the top of his head would not quite coincide with the slope of the adjacent wall. Santana and Pasarell walked past him. Pasarell, his hair falling over his forehead, looked sleepy and impassive. Santana's dark eyes were bright and he was smiling. Applause greeted them, and they began to warm up. Both are fairly large but not impressively or even athletically built. In the way they moved, however, and in the way they hit the ball, they showed, even in warmup, why they were there. "When they win Wimbledon, they win the world," Twynam said. Santana once worked as a ball boy at a club in Madrid. His family had no money. To finance a tennis career, he found a sponsor, and now he has become a national hero in Spain. He is the first Spaniard who has ever won at Wimbledon, and the first tennis player ever to be given an award that the Spanish government annually makes to the nation's outstanding athlete. A touch player, he has been called a genius with a racket, a stylist, a virtuoso, and a master of many shots. He has been said to have thirty-seven shots known to the game and two that no one has ever heard of. He has seven different forehands. When Santana — at the end of the court near Twynam — began to serve in the match with Pasarell, Twynam said, "Santana is a scientific player, very steady. Watch him now, though. Watch his right foot. He drags his toe something shocking, he does." Santana lifted the ball high and swung through for his first serve. His right toe, never coming off the ground, moved in an arc toward the base line and scuffed up the grass. After six or eight serves, Santana had made a light but distinct crescent in the lawn.

Twynam looked at the sky, which was thickening a little but not seriously. "All in all, the Lord has done pretty well for us," he said. Pasarell got ready to serve. Pasarell's father, who is chairman of the board of Philip Morris de Puerto Rico, was once tennis champion of the island. So was Charlie's mother. Charlie grew up in a beautiful house in San Juan and learned his tennis under Welby Van Horn, at the Caribe Hilton. He is very strong, and the dimensions of his game consist of power and more power. He is technically moody, given to flashes of brilliance, and when he is playing well and is fired up he is a beautiful tennis player and almost unbeatable. But his game can fall apart quickly. He relies on speed, the hard ball, the rush to the net. He has four shots: one forehand, one backhand, one serve, and one volley — boom, boom, boom, boom. If he could give Santana any game at all, it would be a contest between power and style. As Pasarell was about to serve, Twynam said, "Watch this one now. Watch his foot." Pasarell tossed the ball into the air and swung through. "See how he lifts that foot?" Twynam went on. "See how he puts it down flat? He's all right, he is. First-class. He doesn't drag his foot."

Santana broke through Pasarell's fourth service and soon led 5–3. Lovely, puffy clouds were now moving swiftly overhead.

"They're all right, but I'd sooner see a nice blue sky," Twynam said. "Beggars can't be choosers, I suppose." The scuff line under Santana's toe was becoming a small rut. "Shocking," Twynam said. "But the court can take it." Pasarell broke back through Santana's service, and the first set went to 8–8 before Pasarell broke through again. He won the set, 10–8.

Taking his time during the next change of ends, Pasarell walked slowly to the umpire's chair, toweled himself, and looked at the sky. Returning to the court, he spoke to himself. "Come on, Charlie," he said. He said this aloud to himself about once a game, all afternoon. He won the second set, 6–3.

The sky had gone gray, and several minutes later a pouring rain fell. "I'm no God," Twynam said. "I can't stop the bloody weather." His crew had the net down and the court covered in sixty seconds. The rain lasted seven more minutes. The cover came off, the net went up, and, less than ten minutes after play had stopped, the match was under way again. "It all has to do with the paying customers," Twynam said, after directing the operation. "If there was no one watching, we wouldn't give two hoots. Let's have another four or five hours of sunshine, God. Be good to us, please." Three minutes later, the sun broke through and patches of blue appeared in the sky. Santana won the third set, 6–2.

It appeared that Santana had found his touch and had turned the match around. Pasarell, however, seemed stronger in the fourth set than he had been all day. He was leading, 4–3, when more rain began to fall. "This has never happened for donkey's years, this," Twynam said. "It's bad for the public, bad for form." Twynam, as it happened, was referring not to the rain, for his crew has covered and uncovered the Centre Court as many as eight times in one afternoon, but to the match itself. In the ninety years of the Wimbledon tournament, no defending champion had ever lost on opening day, and it appeared that the defending champion was in danger of losing now. Fourteen minutes after the new rain had begun, the sun was out again and there were wide blue patches of sky in the west. Breaking Pasarell's service, Santana tied the set, at 5–5. "Come on, Charlie," Pasarell said as he missed the shot that blew the tenth game. Santana won the eleventh, Pasarell the twelfth. Then, in the thirteenth game, Pasarell broke Santana's service. "He's a bit of a rawboned American, but he's getting there," Twynam said. A few minutes later, in bright sunshine, Pasarell chased a lob, running toward the base line, and Santana moved up to the net. Pasarell stopped, turned, and drove the ball past Santana to win the match, 10–8, 6–3, 2–6, 8–6.

"What did you expect?" Twynam said. "He didn't drag his foot."

Ashe

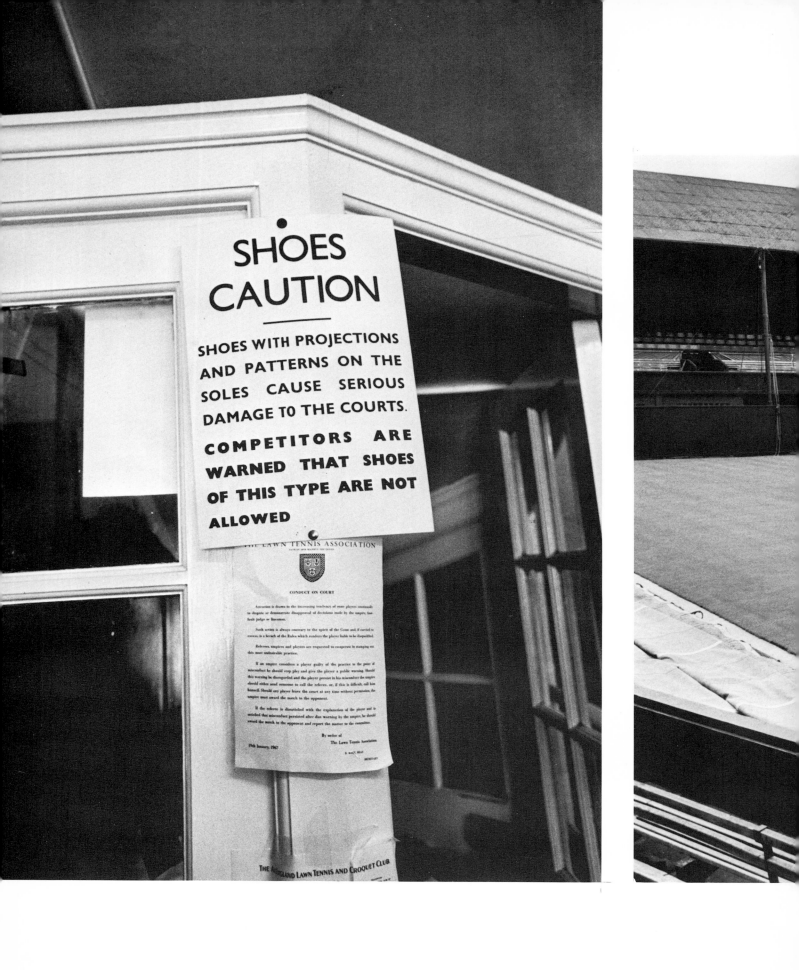

Curtis

Riessen

Kodes   Dell

Laver

◀Niessen   Chanfreau   Centre Court▶

IT
2

PREVIOUS SETS

7 6 2
1 2 3 4
5 1 6

R.G.LAVER

T.S.OKKER

2 5
ER SETS GAM
1 2

Melville   Court ►

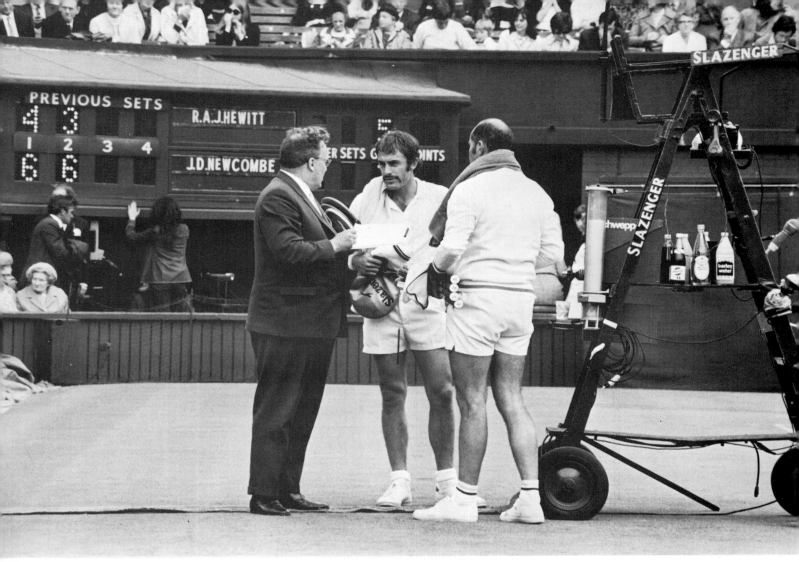

Newcombe   Hewitt

Laver

"A drop of rain, no more—just to give it a drink, just to cool the grass."